Cambridge Elements

Elements of Sustainability: Science, Policy, Practice
edited by
Series Editor-in-Chief
Arun Agrawal
University of Michigan

CLIMATE CHANGE ON TRIAL

Mobilizing Human Rights Litigation to Accelerate Climate Action

César Rodríguez-Garavito
New York University

CAMBRIDGE
UNIVERSITY PRESS

Shaftesbury Road, Cambridge CB2 8EA, United Kingdom

One Liberty Plaza, 20th Floor, New York, NY 10006, USA

477 Williamstown Road, Port Melbourne, VIC 3207, Australia

314–321, 3rd Floor, Plot 3, Splendor Forum, Jasola District Centre,
New Delhi – 110025, India

103 Penang Road, #05–06/07, Visioncrest Commercial, Singapore 238467

Cambridge University Press is part of Cambridge University Press & Assessment, a department of the University of Cambridge.

We share the University's mission to contribute to society through the pursuit of education, learning and research at the highest international levels of excellence.

www.cambridge.org
Information on this title: www.cambridge.org/9781009644327

DOI: 10.1017/9781009420563

© César Rodríguez-Garavito 2025

This publication is in copyright. Subject to statutory exception and to the provisions of relevant collective licensing agreements, with the exception of the Creative Commons version the link for which is provided below, no reproduction of any part may take place without the written permission of Cambridge University Press & Assessment.

An online version of this work is published at doi.org/10.1017/9781009420563 under a Creative Commons Open Access license CC-BY-NC-ND 4.0 which permits re-use, distribution and reproduction in any medium for non-commercial purposes providing appropriate credit to the original work is given. You may not distribute derivative works without permission. To view a copy of this license, visit https://creativecommons.org/licenses/by-nc-nd/4.0

When citing this work, please include a reference to the DOI 10.1017/9781009420563

First published 2025

A catalogue record for this publication is available from the British Library

ISBN 978-1-009-64432-7 Hardback
ISBN 978-1-009-42052-5 Paperback
ISSN 2635-0211 (online)
ISSN 2635-0203 (print)

Additional resources for this publication at www.cambridge.org/climate-change-on-trial

Cambridge University Press & Assessment has no responsibility for the persistence or accuracy of URLs for external or third-party internet websites referred to in this publication and does not guarantee that any content on such websites is, or will remain, accurate or appropriate.

For EU product safety concerns, contact us at Calle de José Abascal, 56, 1°, 28003 Madrid, Spain, or email eugpsr@cambridge.org

Climate Change on Trial

Mobilizing Human Rights Litigation to Accelerate Climate Action

Elements of Sustainability: Science, Policy, Practice

DOI: 10.1017/9781009420563
First published online: May 2025

César Rodríguez-Garavito
New York University
Author for correspondence: César Rodríguez-Garavito,
cesar.rodriguez@nyu.edu

Abstract: This Element tells the twenty-year socio-legal story of human rights-based climate change litigation. Based on an original database of the totality of rights-based climate change (RCC) lawsuits around the world as well as interviews with leading actors and participant observation in the field, the Element explains the rise and global diffusion of RCC litigation. It combines insights from global governance, international law, climate policy, human rights, and legal mobilization theory in order to offer a socio-legal account of the actors, strategies, and norms that have emerged at the intersection of human rights and climate governance. By proposing a broad understanding of the impacts of legal mobilization that includes direct and indirect, material and symbolic effects, it documents the contributions and shortcomings of human rights litigation in addressing the climate emergency.

This title is also available as open access on Cambridge Core.

Keywords: climate change, human rights, climate policy, climate law, environmental law

© César Rodríguez-Garavito 2025

ISBNs: 9781009644327 (HB), 9781009420525 (PB), 9781009420563 (OC)
ISSNs: 2635-0211 (online), 2635-0203 (print)

Contents

1. Introduction: Putting Climate Change on Trial ... 1

2. Explaining the Rights Turn: Legal Opportunities and Mobilizing Frames at the Intersection of Human Rights and Climate Governance ... 11

3. The Shape of the Field: Issues, Venues, Actors, and Strategies in Rights-Based Climate Litigation ... 32

4. Addressing the Unique Challenges of Global Warming: The Evolving Law of Human Rights and Climate Change ... 60

5. The Impact of Rights-Based Climate Litigation: Typology and Illustrations ... 89

6. Looking Ahead: Lessons, Blind Spots, and the Potential of Rights-Based Climate Litigation ... 110

An Online Appendix for this Element is available at www.cambridge.org/climate-change-on-trial

1 Introduction: Putting Climate Change on Trial

Barely a decade ago, the idea of suing governments and corporations for the profound impacts of climate change on human rights was met with skepticism at best and with derision at worst. Legal scholars and practitioners were among the skeptics. Indeed, most legal observers at the outset of the pioneering cases of the early 2010s thought such cases were unlikely to succeed. For instance, when the environmental organization Urgenda sued the Dutch government in 2013 to demand that it increase the ambition of its greenhouse gas (GHG) emissions cuts, many observers assumed the case would be too radical a claim for the courts.[1]

In 2019, the Dutch Supreme Court proved the skeptics wrong: It ruled in favor of Urgenda and the 866 citizens that participated in the case as co-plaintiffs and ordered the government to raise the country's GHG emissions reduction target in line with the prescriptions of the United Nations (UN) Intergovernmental Panel on Climate Change (IPCC) and the goals of the 2015 Paris climate agreement.[2] Crucially, one of the pillars of the court's decision was the recognition that the government's insufficient ambition with regard to climate mitigation violated regional and international human rights duties.

Following this major win, Urgenda went on to establish the Climate Litigation Network in order to advise the growing number of litigants interested in replicating the idea in other jurisdictions. This legal strategy has spread like wildfire. As shown in the full list of cases in the Online Appendix, similar suits have been filed, with mixed results, in Belgium, Canada, the Czech Republic, France, Germany, Ireland, Poland, Romania, Russia, South Korea, Spain, Sweden, Switzerland, and the United Kingdom.[3]

Strikingly, human rights advocates were particularly incredulous about climate litigation. As the lawyers who participated in the pioneering cases recalled in our interviews, initially human rights organizations were indifferent and even hostile to the possibility of framing global warming as a human rights issue, let alone going to court over it. For instance, in 2003, when the attorney Paul Crowley was working with the Indigenous leader Sheila Watt-Cloutier and the attorneys Donald Goldberg (Center for International Environmental Law, CIEL) and Martin Wagner (Earthjustice) on their legal petition against the United States government before the Inter-American Commission on Human

---

[1] Interview with Tessa Khan, the former director of the Climate Litigation Network (CLN). (Transcripts of all interviews are on file with the author.)
[2] Case 29. For the sake of brevity and clarity, I identify the cases in the footnotes by their chronological numbering in the Online Appendix.
[3] See, respectively, Cases 40, 86, 224, 84, 87, 63, 204, 329, 292, 146, 156, 298, 52, and 71.

Rights (IACHR) – the first-ever case seeking to hold a government accountable for human rights violations stemming from global warming – they tried to collaborate with some of the largest human rights international nongovernmental organizations (INGOs). They did not get far, as those groups failed to see global warming as a human rights problem. In fact, human rights INGOs tended to view the application of human rights norms to climate change as a distraction – a potential overextension of the rights frame that would take attention away from violations of civil and political rights. In Crowley's words, "pretty well [the] universal reaction we got from the traditional groups was ... *those* aren't human rights, *these* are human rights – it's individuals who are being tortured, who are in prison, that's what this is about and you're diluting that by lumping everything into this [human rights] discourse."[4]

The legal profession in countries like the United States tended to see the idea as far-fetched. "People thought it was *crazy*," said Kelly Matheson, Deputy Director of Global Climate Litigation at Our Children's Trust (OCT), referring to OCT's initiative to sue the United States' federal and state governments in the early 2010s for contributing to the climate emergency in a way that allegedly violated young people's basic rights as well as their obligation to hold the natural environment in trust for their citizens.[5]

I remember the skepticism beginning to subside around the time that I first participated in discussions among climate and human rights scholars and advocates. At a closed-door workshop at the University of São Paulo in 2016, human rights organizations like Conectas, environmental organizations like Greenpeace, and children's rights collectives like Alana came together to discuss the feasibility of filing a rights-based climate lawsuit in Brazil. Encouraged by the success of *Urgenda* in the first instance of the case (including a favorable ruling from The Hague District Court in 2015), as well as by OCT's filing of its first federal case on behalf of young people (*Juliana* v. *United States*) in 2015, workshop participants began to lay the legal groundwork and forge the ties of collaboration that would be needed to pursue climate cases in Brazil. Although the process would take four more years and a second event where we reconvened in São Paulo in 2019, some of those organizations would go on to file one of the pioneering lawsuits of this sort in 2020. The *Climate Fund* case challenged the Bolsonaro administration's anti-environmental policies, specifically its decision not to implement a law that had established a fund to finance climate mitigation and anti-deforestation programs in the Amazon region. In

---

[4] Interview with Paul Crowley, Sheila Watt-Cloutier's lawyer in the Inuit petition to the IACHR (emphasis in original).

[5] Interview with Kelly Matheson, Deputy Director of Global Climate Litigation at OCT (emphasis in original).

ruling for the plaintiffs in 2022, Brazil's Supreme Court (Supremo Tribunal Federal) advanced what is perhaps the most categorical articulation that any supreme court has offered of climate change as a human rights issue. By declaring that "there are no human rights on a dead or sick planet" and that "environmental law treaties constitute a subset of human rights treaties," the Supreme Court accorded the Paris Agreement the supra-legal status that human rights treaties have in Brazilian constitutional law.[6] The filing of *Climate Fund* helped open the door to a spate of cases that has turned Brazil into one of the most active jurisdictions for this sort of litigation anywhere in the world.

Two decades after the Inuit petition before the IACHR, twelve years after the filing of *Urgenda*, and almost a decade after that initial workshop in São Paulo, rights-based climate change (RCC) litigation has moved from the margins to the mainstream. In a single month in 2024, the two leading international human rights courts – the European Court of Human Rights (ECtHR) and the Inter-American Court of Human Rights (IACtHR) – gave their stamp of approval to what scholars have called the "rights turn" in climate litigation.[7] A few weeks after the ECtHR handed down its first climate ruling – declaring that Switzerland's insufficient climate policies had violated the rights of elderly women who are particularly vulnerable to extreme heat[8] – the IACtHR heard from lawyers, scientists, advocates, and youth leaders from across the Americas at a three-day hearing in Barbados, the first of three that the Court convened as part of the process leading to its advisory opinion on climate change and human rights. For those of us presenting to the Court and answering the probing questions of the robed judges, it seemed that climate change itself was on trial.

Between January 2005 and December 2024, a total of 467 RCC cases have been filed in 50 national courts and 13 regional and international courts and quasi-judicial bodies. This rights turn has been particularly salient since the mid 2010s. Indeed, 93 percent of cases have been filed since 2015. A wide range of scholarly, advocacy, scientific, journalistic, and funding initiatives have emerged to undertake, document, report, or support this type of legal action.

This Element tells the socio-legal story of this field. Theoretically, it combines insights from global governance, international relations, international law, and legal mobilization studies in order to offer an account of RCC litigation.

---

[6] Case 151 (*Partido Socialista Brasileiro (PSB), Partido Socialismo e Liberdade (PSOL), Partido dos Trabalhadores (PT) e Rede Sustentabilidade v. União Federal*, ADPF 708, at 8 (July 4, 2022)).

[7] Peel, Jacqueline and Osofsky, Hari M. 2018. "A Rights Turn in Climate Litigation?" *Transnational Environmental Law* 7 (1): 37–67; Savaresi, Annalisa and Setzer, Joana. 2022. "Rights-Based Litigation in the Climate Emergency: Mapping the Landscape and New Knowledge Frontiers." *Journal of Human Rights and the Environment* 13 (1): 7–34.

[8] Case 52.

Empirically, it draws from a combination of sources, including a systematic compilation and analysis of all RCC cases filed before national and international judicial and quasi-judicial bodies, semi-structured interviews with litigants and other key actors in RCC litigation, and participant observation in court hearings, strategy meetings, and public events with RCC actors around the world.

As lawsuits have proliferated, so too have scholarly studies on them. However, the literature on this type of legal mobilization – that is, the mobilization of human rights law and litigation to advance climate action – consists mostly of accounts of one case or a few particularly successful cases.[9] In the absence of systematic, theoretically informed analyses of RCC litigation, we lack a comprehensive understanding of its origins, legal doctrines, and practical effects. This Element seeks to contribute to filling this gap by studying the universe of RCC cases and offering an analytical account of the rise, trajectory, and results of RCC litigation. In terms of international law and international relations theory, it views RCC litigation as a "transnational legal process,"[10] that is, as an iterative set of interactions among a wide range of public, private, and civil society actors who formulate, interpret, disseminate, and internalize new norms about the human rights implications of climate change. As RCC lawsuits and rulings have proliferated and articulated new legal norms around the world, the rights turn has given rise to a "norm cascade"[11] with tangible impacts on climate governance.

This Element also seeks to address another gap in the existing literature. Just as environmental lawyers spearheaded RCC litigation and human rights advocates only later came on board, environmental law and governance scholars have been at the forefront of studies on the matter, with human rights scholars having played a less active role thus far. This asymmetry has resulted in two analytical gaps. First, we have a considerably better understanding of one aspect of RCC litigation (that is, its impact on climate governance) than the other (that is, its effect on human rights norms and concepts). In reality, however, RCC litigation has shaped (and been shaped by) international human rights as much as it has shaped climate governance. As RCC litigants, judges, advocates, UN specialists, and other norm entrepreneurs have reframed global warming as a rights issue and thus influenced climate governance, they have also had an impact on the human rights field by advancing new doctrines such as the rights

---

[9] For a survey of the literature remarking on this limitation of climate litigation studies, see Setzer, Joana and Vanhala, Lisa C. 2019. "Climate Change Litigation: A Review of Research on Courts and Litigants in Climate Governance." *WIREs Climate Change* 10 (3): 1.

[10] Koh, Harold. 1996. "The 1994 Roscoe Pound Lecture: Transnational Legal Process." *Nebraska Law Review* 75 (1): 181–207; Finnemore, Martha and Sikkink, Kathryn. 1998. "International Norm Dynamics and Political Change." *International Organization* 52 (4): 887–917.

[11] Finnemore and Sikkink, *supra* note 10.

of future generations and the right to a stable climate system. Therefore, this Element investigates developments in both the climate governance field *and* the human rights field in order to examine their two-way relationship and hybridization.

Second, since environmental governance scholars have had the leading role in the study of RCC litigation, the literature on the matter has yet to fully incorporate insights from human rights scholarship that are directly relevant to understanding climate litigation. I contribute to filling this gap by applying lessons from the rich literature on the emergence and dissemination of other fields of human rights norms and advocacy that predated RCC litigation, such as socioeconomic rights.

In engaging equally with these two bodies of knowledge and practice, I intend to offer analytical tools and empirical evidence that question the view that the climate and the human rights global regimes are stuck in a dysfunctional equilibrium and that very little can change in both fields.[12] While RCC litigation certainly falls short of the speed and scale of legal transformation that are required to deal with the climate emergency, and while I dwell on its blind spots and shortfalls, I also show how new rights frames and norms have emerged and cascaded in a relatively short period of time – one that even RCC norm entrepreneurs, let alone the skeptics of the early years, could not have anticipated. Contrary to sweeping statements about the "end times" of human rights, I show how the climate emergency, one of the crucial challenges of our time, has been effectively reframed as a human rights issue.[13]

Sheila Watt-Cloutier, the Indigenous leader who spearheaded the Inuit petition, rightly noted that, despite being dismissed by the IACHR, the case succeeded in bringing the attention of the world to the climate emergency and the plight of the Inuit. The public visibility and impact of the case took her and her lawyers by surprise. "We had cast our line to see what fish we would catch, and instead we caught a whale," she wrote.[14] This Element is an attempt to illustrate how dynamic and contingent transnational legal processes can be even when it comes to dealing with the most complex planetary challenges like climate change. At a time when whales – both literal and figurative – are endangered, it shows that they still exist.

---

[12] See, among others, Moyn, Samuel. 2019. *Not Enough: Human Rights in an Unequal World*. Cambridge, MA: Belknap Press; Sachs, Noah M. 2020. "The Paris Agreement in the 2020s: Breakdown or Breakup?" *Ecology Law Quarterly* 46 (1): 865–909.

[13] See Hopgood, Stephen. 2013. *The Endtimes of Human Rights*. Ithaca, NY: Cornell University Press. For an evidence-based critique of this view, see Dancy, Geoff and Christopher Farris. 2023. "The Global Resonance of Human Rights: What Google Search Can Tell." *American Political Science Review* 118 (1): 252–273.

[14] Watt-Cloutier, Sheila. 2015. *The Right to Be Cold*. Minneapolis: University of Minnesota Press, at 230.

1.1 The Argument of the Element

This Element asks the following questions: What accounts for the rights turn in climate litigation? What norms are emerging from this transnational legal process? What are the impacts and limitations of this type of legal action in advancing climate action? Drawing on theories of global governance and legal mobilization, I argue that the rights turn was enabled by the eventual convergence of two very different and distinct global regulatory regimes – climate governance and human rights – that had developed largely along parallel tracks until the mid 2010s. The fresh legal opportunities and additional mobilization frames made available by this convergence facilitated the rise of RCC litigation. They also produced an array of legal norms in this growing field of practice, as well as tangible impacts on climate policy and movements. Although the lead-up to the 2015 Conference of the Parties (COP) of the United Nations Framework Convention on Climate Change (UNFCCC) – and the resulting Paris Agreement – served as the focal point for this convergence, the legal norms and the framing of climate change as a human rights issue originated in longer-term processes, namely the gradual incorporation of environmental issues into the international human rights regime, on one hand, and the revamping of the climate regime that followed the failure of the 1998 Kyoto Protocol and led to the adoption of the Paris Agreement, on the other.

The Paris Agreement is the first global climate accord to explicitly recognize the relevance of human rights in climate action. But rather than its (relatively weak) language on rights, the Agreement's role in catalyzing RCC litigation lies in the *legal opportunities* associated with its structure. While the Kyoto Protocol established mandatory targets and timetables for (developed) states' emissions cuts, the Paris Agreement allows states to determine their own non-binding individual emissions reduction targets. Under the Paris Agreement, climate outcomes depend on states periodically reviewing and increasing their contributions through a "Pledge and Review" iterative process. Currently, even if all states complied with the pledges they made pursuant to the Paris Agreement the planet would almost certainly still warm by about 2.3°C.[15] This would be dire for the world and could, among other impacts, force as many as a billion people to migrate by 2050 and diminish per capita economic output by between 15 percent and 25 percent by 2100, a trough as deep as the depression of the 1930s.[16] Collective ambition within the international

---

[15] Emissions Gap Report 2024: No More Hot Air ... Please!, United Nations Environment Programme, 2024, available at: http://bit.ly/40sARCg, at 34.

[16] For information on the impact of global warming on migration, see "Migration, Environment and Climate Change: Assessing the Evidence," International Organization for Migration [IOM], 2009. Available at: http://bit.ly/3zFLlEE. On the economic impact of climate change, see

community must increase accordingly: The current policy trajectory would result in emissions at an estimated 57 percent higher in 2035 than needed to achieve the Agreement's goal of limiting global warming to 1.5°C and to avoid the more extreme scenarios of climate change.[17]

With planet-warming emissions still on the rise and the large majority of states missing even their grossly insufficient targets, incentives for states to carry out and upwardly revise their contributions need to come not only from peer pressure (at the international periodic reporting and stocktaking meetings envisaged by the Paris Agreement) but also from domestic civil society pressure, including through litigation. As Keohane and Oppenheimer conclude, "the climate outcomes after Paris [follow] from what can be characterized as a 'two-level game', involving a combination of international strategic interaction and domestic politics."[18]

Based on evidence from the totality of RCC lawsuits, I argue that litigants have sought to leverage this two-level structure of opportunities for legal mobilization by (1) asking courts to take the *goals and principles of the climate regime* (as laid out in the Paris Agreement and IPCC reports) as benchmarks to assess governments' (and, to a lesser extent, corporations') climate actions and omissions and (2) invoking *the norms, frames, and enforcement mechanisms of human rights* to hold them legally accountable to such goals and principles and thus accelerate climate action.

Indeed, most rights-based lawsuits explicitly integrate the standards and regulatory logic of the climate regime, notably the Paris Agreement and the IPCC assessments (as updated by the quickly evolving and improving climate science). This type of RCC litigation can provide *material* incentives for governments to overcome policy gridlock, increase compliance and ambition, and foster transparency and participation in climate policy. Further, by publicly reframing the problem of climate change as a source of grievous impacts on identifiable human beings and as a violation of universally recognized norms, it can create *symbolic* incentives for governments and other domestic actors to align their actions with the goals of the global climate regime.

The failure of international diplomacy to produce even modest progress on climate action has exposed the enforcement gaps of the Paris Agreement and prompted a slew of lawsuits that aim to fill some of those gaps – and,

---

Marshall Burke et al. 2018. "Large Potential Reduction in Economic Damages under UN Mitigation Targets." *Nature* 557: 549–553, 549; see also Wallace-Wells, David. 2019. *The Uninhabitable Earth: Life after Warming*. New York: Random House, at 122.

[17] Emissions Gap Report 2024: No More Hot Air ... Please!, *supra* note 15, at 32.
[18] Keohane, Robert O. and Oppenheimer, Michael. 2016. "Paris: Beyond the Climate Dead End through Pledge and Review?" *Politics and Governance* 4 (3): 142–151, 148.

increasingly, go beyond the Paris framework. However, climate change is too complex a problem for any single regulatory tactic to adequately address. Rights-based litigation is only one tool in a broader governance toolkit that involves a wide array of actors and approaches, including government representatives engaged in periodic negotiations around the UNFCCC, grassroots activists protesting on the streets to demand climate action and justice, scientists refining the data and sounding the alarm on global warming and its impacts on humans and nonhumans, corporate actors contributing to the transition to clean energies, and so on. RCC litigation has its own challenges and blind spots, including insufficient attention to climate adaptation and reparations as well as the limitations of human rights norms in dealing with the complex causality and temporality of global warming.

1.2 The Element's Structure and Methodology

The remainder of the Element is divided into five sections. Section 2 places the legal stock and frames of RCC litigation in the context of longer-term processes within the human rights and climate governance regimes – namely, the incorporation of environmental rights into international human rights and comparative constitutional law, on one hand, and the regulatory convergence in the climate regime around the Paris Agreement and the IPCC's scientific assessments, on the other. Section 3 takes a deep dive into RCC litigation. The first part of the section offers a typology of cases, documents their thematic and regional distribution, and tracks their evolution and results. The second part characterizes the RCC field by examining its actors as well as their roles and interactions. Section 4 offers an analysis of the legal norms and doctrines emerging from RCC lawsuits and court decisions. Although it is too early to make hard and fast inferences about the individual and aggregate impacts of RCC cases, Section 5 proposes a typology of impacts and offers preliminary evidence based on case studies of four of the most prominent lawsuits of this sort. Section 6 recaps the argument, the evidence, and the conclusions about the potential contributions and challenges of RCC litigation in advancing climate action.

A final word on methods: As noted, this Element's empirical point of departure is the systematic compilation and analysis of an original database of all the RCC cases that have been brought before judicial bodies (including domestic, regional, and global courts) and quasi-judicial bodies (including national human rights commissions and UN human rights treaty bodies). Following the convention in the literature, the list includes cases in which the terms "climate change" and "rights" appear explicitly in the petition or the judicial decision.[19] The cutoff date is December 31, 2024. The database was compiled and is regularly updated by the research team that I lead at New York University School of Law's Climate Law Accelerator (CLX). The database is available to the public on CLX's website.[20] In order to maximize the chance of capturing the totality of relevant cases, we use a triangulation of sources, including the comprehensive databases on climate litigation curated by Columbia University's Sabin Center and LSE's Grantham Research Institute on Climate Change and the Environment. Our narrower focus on rights-based litigation allows us to carry out a more granular search that identifies additional cases through a combination of internet searches, reading of secondary materials, and interviews with expert informants. Given the explosion and global diffusion of this sort of litigation, our database, just like other well-established databases, needs to be constantly complemented and updated and is likely to miss a few cases at any given time.

In addition to the analysis of the texts of all the petitions and rulings that are available online, this study is based on formal semi-structured interviews with a range of key actors in RCC litigation. The list of interviewees includes litigants, advocates, media experts, climate negotiators, human rights and environmental law NGO leaders, UN special rapporteurs, youth and Indigenous activists, and funders from around the world who have participated in or supported RCC cases.

I also draw on evidence from almost a decade of participant observation in in-person and online meetings and events with actors in the RCC field. In my capacity as a legal scholar and occasional participant in litigation, I have had the opportunity to participate in strategy meetings, court hearings, expert consultations, public panels, trainings, community consultations, and other convenings in venues as diverse as the annual COPs, Indigenous territories in the Amazon, the headquarters of the UN Human Rights Council in Geneva, and communities of climate refugees in Bangladesh. I have also conducted fieldwork with plaintiffs, lawyers, judges, and other relevant actors in a number of countries, including Argentina, Australia, Bangladesh, Barbados, Brazil, Canada, Colombia, Dominica, Ecuador, Germany, India, Italy, Kenya, Mexico, New Zealand, the Netherlands, Norway, Peru, South Africa, Spain, the United Kingdom, and the United States.

---

[19] Rodríguez-Garavito, César. 2022. "Litigating the Climate Emergency: The Global Rise of Human Rights–Based Litigation for Climate Action." In *Litigating the Climate Emergency*, edited by César Rodríguez-Garavito. Cambridge: Cambridge University Press: 9–83; Peel and Osofsky, *supra* note 7.

[20] Climate Law Accelerator (CLX) Toolkit. "Case Database." Available at: https://clxtoolkit.com/map/.

This triangulation of methods combines an external and an internal perspective on this dynamic field of study and practice. I take a step back (or two) from the intense pace and the particularities of any given case in order to offer a global picture of RCC litigation and explain its origins, norms, effects, and shortcomings with the help of concepts and theories from global governance, international law, international relations, and legal mobilization.

This view, however, risks missing the richness of the transnational legal process that underlies it: the myriad local and international actors that participate in it; the social interactions through which new strategies and norms are constructed; the high-paced learning and cross-fertilization among litigants and judges located in very different jurisdictions; and the impact that RCC litigation is having on a range of places and actors, from the climate movement to corporate boards to diplomats and human rights organizations. Therefore, I draw on in-depth interviews and participant observation to offer a more granular, ethnographic view of RCC litigation. This is reflected in vignettes, stories, and deep dives into specific cases that the reader will find throughout the Element.

I would like to think that the combination of numbers, concepts, and stories provides a nuanced account of the use of human rights and courts to address the climate emergency – one that does justice to its notable achievements while also capturing its fits and starts, serendipitous evolution, and open questions. Once a legal or political strategy catches on, it is tempting for analysts and practitioners to see it as an inevitable development and focus on studying or promoting its replication around the world. To counter this temptation, I seek to capture the experimental nature of RCC litigation, including its uncertainties, learning processes, and multifarious outcomes.

This sense of experimentation was there from the beginning. At a side panel in Milan during the 2003 COP, Sheila Watt-Cloutier, Paul Crowley, and Donald Goldberg addressed a crowd that spilled into the hallway. As Watt-Cloutier recounts, in announcing the filing of their petition before the IACHR, "we described the changing reality of Inuit life and the human suffering that accompanied the melting Arctic. The audience responded enthusiastically. The power of the rights-based approach was that it moved the discussion out of the realm of dry economic and technical debate that too often overtakes discussion at UN climate change conferences."[21] The reframing of global warming as a human rights issue became even clearer to the Inuit leader during an interview after the event, when she realized that her claim and that of her people could be described as "the right to be cold." Two decades later, at a time of record-breaking heat

---

[21] Watt-Cloutier, *supra* note 14.

waves and unprecedented forest fires, we will embark on a journey into the legal experiment that made the right to be cold, and the new norms it entails, a universal human rights cause.

2 Explaining the Rights Turn: Legal Opportunities and Mobilizing Frames at the Intersection of Human Rights and Climate Governance

On a sunny morning in December 2023, Luís Roberto Barroso, Chief Justice of the Brazilian Supreme Court, addressed a panel of judges and a global audience of legal experts who had gathered in the packed conference room at the Dubai Expo where COP28 was held, as well as in the online room that the United Nations Environment Programme (UNEP) set up for the occasion. Drawing on case law from around the world and his own opinion in the *Climate Fund* ruling, Barroso opened his presentation with a confident assessment of the status of rights-based climate jurisprudence. To begin with, why should courts get involved in RCC cases? Barroso offered three reasons. First, "the protection of the environment and fighting climate change is now being perceived as an autonomous fundamental right, as has been recognized by the Inter-American Court of Human Rights."[22] He was alluding to the IACtHR's 2017 advisory opinion, which had indeed framed environmental protection and climate action as human rights duties. Second, courts need to intervene to redress and prevent climate-induced human rights violations given that "majoritarian politics does not have the proper incentive to move because they have short-term objectives."[23] And third, according to the Chief Justice, judges "need to protect those who do not have vote or voice: we are talking about children, we are talking about the next generation, we are talking about people who have not been born yet."[24]

Barroso's nuanced arguments evinced his long experience as a constitutional law scholar and practitioner. A casual observer could have missed their significance, instead seeing them as a rehashing of classic defenses of judicial activism in the face of government inaction. However, for those of us in the room who had followed the evolution of RCC litigation over the years, his remarks and the circumstances of his talk were anything but ordinary. After all, less than a decade earlier, the proposal to incorporate human rights language into international climate law had been met with such reticence that the Paris Agreement resulting from COP21 made only a passing mention of human rights in its preamble. And exactly twenty years had passed from COP9 in Milan, where the

---

[22] Transcript from event "Climate Change and Courts: Judicial Perspectives on Climate Litigation," December 10, 2023. Dubai, UAE.
[23] Ibid. [24] Ibid.

idea of filing an RCC case was so novel that it was treated like breaking news by the media, as we saw in the previous section.

Unlike the event that Sheila Watt-Cloutier and her lawyers had to organize in side rooms to present the Inuit petition, the Dubai panel was a major event at the heart of COP, co-sponsored by UNEP, the Global Judicial Institute on the Environment (GJIE), the International Union for Conservation of Nature (IUCN) World Commission on Environmental Law, and other global organizations. The panel featured chief justices and high court judges who spoke about climate law and jurisprudence, oftentimes quoting from landmark judicial decisions from jurisdictions on the other side of the world from theirs. I attended the event as the director of New York University (NYU) Law's Climate Law Accelerator, which co-sponsored the panel as well as a full-day academic dialogue on climate science and law co-organized with the GJIE. The dialogue brought together climate scientists and legal scholars with judges from supreme and high courts from Brazil, Kenya, Nepal, Pakistan, and South Africa, as well as a judge of the International Court of Justice.

At both events, the judges posed sharp questions and offered thought-provoking insights on climate law issues, from standing and remedies to causality and extraterritorial responsibilities. Watching them and participating in their conversations, it was impossible to miss how much had changed in only twenty years, which is a relatively short period in the slow evolution of international and comparative law. In a clear sign that the RCC field had reached its maturity, high-level judges, who are understandably reluctant to engage publicly with emergent legal questions, were visibly comfortable and indeed keen to speak about climate change as a fundamental human rights issue that required decisive action, including by courts.

How did RCC litigation go from being dismissed by many to a safe topic for dialogue and debate among prominent judges? How did it move from the periphery to the legal mainstream?

2.1 An Unlikely Convergence

The convergence of climate governance and human rights was not a foregone conclusion. Rather, it is a remarkable development, given the litany of failed efforts to create linkages between human rights and climate action and the reluctance of major human rights organizations to take on climate change.[25]

For a quarter of a century, human rights and climate change evolved along distinct and parallel tracks. Before the mid 2010s, no international

---

[25] Lock, Rebecca and Vanhala, Lisa. 2022. "International NGOs and the (Non) Mobilization of Human Rights in the Context of Climate Change: An Inconvenient Frame?" In *Legal*

climate agreement incorporated rights-based language, nor did any UN human rights instrument or domestic court decision frame climate harms as human rights violations, despite mounting scientific evidence on the massive impact of global warming on human life, bodily integrity, property, health, and other basic needs that have been universally recognized as human rights.

The trajectory of both regulatory regimes reflects this reluctance to link human rights and climate change. The 1992 UN Conference on Environment and Development avoided any mention of rights in the Rio Declaration on sustainable development, as did the UNFCCC, the centerpiece of the global climate regime.[26] In 1994, the UN Human Rights Commission, then the UN's main human rights body, rejected a draft declaration on human rights and the environment that incorporated "the right to a secure, healthy and ecologically sound environment."[27]

It would take fourteen more years for the UN Human Rights Council (which replaced the Human Rights Commission in 2006) to take on climate change. It did so at the request of the Maldives, the first state to frame global warming as a threat to human rights "to show the world the immediate and compelling human face of climate change," in the words of then Foreign Affairs Minister, Abdulla Shahid.[28] The Council requested that the UN High Commissioner for Human Rights conduct the first systematic report on the impact of climate change on human rights.[29] Even then, the highest-ranking UN officer responsible for promoting human rights expressed ambiguity about the legal linkage. The Commissioner's report concluded that "while climate change has obvious implications for the enjoyment of human rights, it is less obvious whether, and to what extent, such effects can be qualified as human rights violations in a strict legal sense."[30]

Against this background, the relatively rapid convergence between human rights and international climate governance since the mid 2010s is a striking turn of events. In 2015, the Paris Agreement included a reference to human rights considerations in its preamble. One year later, a report by

---

Mobilization for Human Rights, edited by Gráinne de Búrca. Oxford: Oxford University Press: 51–C.4N.

[26] Shelton, Dinah. 1993. "What Happened in Rio to Human Rights?" *Yearbook of International Environmental Law* 3 (1): 75–93.

[27] Knox, John H. 2020. "Constructing the Human Right to a Healthy Environment." In *Annual Review of Law and Social Science* 16: 79–95.

[28] Knox, John H. 2014. "Climate Ethics and Human Rights." In *Human Rights and the Environment* 5 (0): 22–34.

[29] Human Rights Council Res. 7/23, UN Doc. A/63/53, 136, March 28, 2008.

[30] Human Rights Council, Annual Report of the UN High Commissioner for Human Rights 2009 Report on the Relationship Between Climate Change and Human Rights. UN Doc. A/HRC/10/61.

the first UN Special Rapporteur on Human Rights and the Environment, a position created in 2015, spelled out in detail the substantive and procedural human rights obligations that states, as a matter of international law, have with regard to climate change.[31] In 2019, the second Rapporteur went beyond his predecessor by publishing a report on climate and human rights that asserted the "right to a safe climate" and made concrete recommendations for governments to end humanity's "addiction to fossil fuels."[32] And in 2021, the UN Human Rights Commission institutionalized the convergence by creating a dedicated Special Rapporteurship on human rights in the context of climate change.

How did human rights and climate change go from diverging to converging? And how does that convergence feed into the ongoing wave of RCC litigation? I tackle these questions with the conceptual tools of legal mobilization theory – that is, the use of the law by social movements and other actors to promote social change.[33] Studies of legal mobilization single out two factors that influence social movements' decision to use litigation and other law-centered strategies: (1) the structure of legal opportunities and (2) the availability of law-centered frames of mobilization. Legal opportunity structures include international and domestic substantive norms (the "legal stock" on the relevant issue area) as well as procedural norms on access to justice that may facilitate or hinder bringing claims to court.[34] Mobilization frames are mental schemata that codify the experience of a social problem (like global warming) through legal categories (like human rights) and offer an organized way of perceiving and responding to the problem.[35] Together with litigants' own resources, these two factors help explain the rise and outcomes of legal mobilization.

---

[31] Knox, John. 2016. "Report of the Special Rapporteur on the Issue of Human Rights Obligations Relating to the Enjoyment of a Safe, Clean, Healthy and Sustainable Environment." UN Doc. A/HRC/31/52, February 1, 2016.

[32] Boyd, David R. 2019. "Report of the Special Rapporteur on the Issue of Human Rights Obligations Relating to the Enjoyment of a Safe, Clean, Healthy and Sustainable Environment." Safe Climate Report, A/74/161, ¶75, July 15, 2019, available at: https://undocs.org/en/A/74/161.

[33] For an overview of legal mobilization scholarship, see McCann, Michael. 2008. "Litigation and Legal Mobilization." In *The Oxford Handbook of Law and Politics*, edited by Gregory A. Caldeira et al. Oxford: Oxford University Press: 522–540.

[34] Legal opportunity structures are a sub-set of political opportunity structures for social mobilization. For a classic formulation of political opportunity theory, see McAdam, Douglas et al. 1996. *Comparative Perspectives on Social Movements: Political Opportunities, Mobilizing Structures, and Cultural Framings*. Cambridge: Cambridge University Press.

[35] Snow, David A. et al. 1986. "Frame Alignment Processes, Micromobilization, and Movement Participation." In *American Sociological Review* 51: 464–481.

The norms and frames that are evident in RCC lawsuits and rulings resulted from internal developments in the human rights and climate governance regimes, namely the mainstreaming of environmental rights in international and constitutional law, on the one hand, and the turn toward a more experimentalist approach in climate governance, on the other. In what follows, I analyze each process in turn. In line with constructivist approaches to international law and international relations, I adopt a dynamic and broad view of norms. As Finnemore and Hollis argue, "norms have an inherently dynamic character; they continuously develop via ongoing processes in which actors extend or amend their meaning as circumstances evolve."[36] This process-centered perspective focuses on "*how* norms evolve, spread and affect behavior."[37] Here, norms are understood broadly as "expectations for the proper behavior of actors with a given identity"[38] – in our case, expectations about public and private actors' behavior with regards to addressing the climate emergency in ways that are consistent with human rights. Importantly, this means that norms may or may not have the status of legal rules. Oftentimes, the legal standards of emergent global regimes (such as climate governance) are first formulated as norms before they are codified into law through global agreements, national legislation, court rulings, or other means. This has been the case with some of the key legal rules stemming from RCC litigation, such as states' duty to increase the ambition of their climate mitigation targets in order to protect the rights of young and future generations.

In documenting developments in international environmental rights and climate governance that created suitable conditions for RCC litigation, I use Finnemore and Sikkink's well-known account of the norm life cycle.[39] I investigate how new norms have emerged, how they have been debated and disseminated (and how they eventually "cascaded") around the world, and whether and how they have been internalized by the relevant actors (that is, whether and how they have gained a taken-for-granted status).[40] I also examine the extent to which they have been incorporated into international and domestic law (be it soft law or hard law), and how the convergence between environmental rights and climate governance constitutes an instance of what Harold Koh calls a "transnational legal process" that set the stage for the reframing of climate change as a human rights issue.[41]

---

[36] Finnemore, Martha and Hollis, Duncan B. 2016. "Constructing Norms for Global Cybersecurity." *American Journal of International Law* 110 (3): 425–479, 428.

[37] Ibid, p. 429 (emphasis in original).

[38] Ibid, citing Katzenstein, Peter J. 1996. "Introduction: Alternative Perspectives on National Security." In *The Culture of National Security: Norms and Identity in World Politics*, edited by Peter J. Katzenstein. New York: Columbia University Press, at 1, 5.

[39] Finnemore and Sikkink, *supra* note 10, 895.   [40] Ibid.   [41] Koh, *supra* note 10.

2.2 The Environmental Rights Cascade and Legal Opportunities for Climate Litigation

2.2.1 Forging a New Right: The International Right to a Healthy Environment

Legal opportunities for the rights turn in climate litigation resulted partly from the broader, longer-term process of convergence between human rights and environmental governance. This process approximates a norm cascade, as one country after another added a right to a healthy environment to its constitution, and international human rights law eventually followed suit.[42] To date, at least 164 countries have recognized a legally binding right to a healthy environment in constitutions, legislation, and treaties, and only 32 have not.[43]

At the global scale, this norm cascade reached its tipping point with the 2021 UN Human Rights Council and the 2022 UN General Assembly resolutions recognizing "the right to a clean, healthy and sustainable environment as a human right."[44] This new universal right was the result of a two-decade process of norm creation. Among the key norm entrepreneurs were states such as Costa Rica, the Maldives, and Switzerland, as well as NGOs like CIEL, Earthjustice, and the Universal Rights Group. Interestingly, this process intersected in unexpected ways with the emergence of specific norms on *climate* and human rights.

Historically, states in both the Global North and the Global South believed that environmental and human rights issues should be kept as entirely separate fields of global governance. This conviction was clearly on display in the first debates on human rights and the environment that took place at the UN Human Rights Commission (the predecessor to the Council) in the mid 1990s. Starting in 1994, the Commission considered a series of proposals on the matter which, for different reasons, faced stiff resistance from leading countries from both the Global North and the Global South and ended in underwhelming Commission resolutions that effectively thwarted this initial attempt to link environmental and human rights governance at the global scale.[45]

---

[42] Finnemore and Sikkink, *supra* note 10.

[43] Author's calculation, building on Boyd, David R. 2018. "Catalyst for Change: Evaluating Forty Years of Experience in Implementing the Right to a Healthy Environment." In *The Human Right to a Healthy Environment*, edited by Knox, John H. & Pejan, Ramin. Cambridge: Cambridge University Press: 17–41.

[44] On UN General Assembly Resolution A/76/L.75, see UN Environment Programme. 2022. "In historic move, UN declares healthy environment a human right," July 28, 2022. Available at: bit.ly/3SePdTo. On UN Human Rights Council Resolution 48/13, see Human Rights Council Res. 48/13, UN Doc. A/HRC/RES/48/13.

[45] Human Rights Commission Res. 1994/65, UN Doc. E/CN.4/RES/1994/65, March 9, 1994; Human Rights Commission Res. 1995/14, UN Doc. E/CN.4/1995/176, January 30 to

The environmental rights normative cascade was ultimately unleashed by specific concerns about climate change, which had become an existential threat to a number of Global South countries by the mid 2000s. Island countries like the small Pacific Island nations and the Philippines brought the issue of climate change and human rights to the newly established UN Human Rights Council.[46]

The first step in this direction was the adoption by consensus of Council Resolution 7/23 in 2008. This was the first UN resolution to acknowledge that global warming raises "an immediate and far-reaching threat to people and communities around the world and has implications for the full enjoyment of human rights."[47] It also requested that the Office of the High Commissioner for Human Rights (OHCHR) prepare the aforementioned 2009 report on the matter.[48] The report was later followed by Council Resolution 10/4 in March 2009, which took note of the report's findings and called for the organization of a panel discussion on climate change and human rights, which took place during the Council session of June 2009.

After that point, it became clear that political differences would stall further progress on climate and human rights at the Council, which led some norm entrepreneurs in government and civil society to conclude that the way out of this impasse would be a two-pronged strategy. First, they sought to build the climate–rights link into the *climate governance* regime. This resulted in the first mention of human rights in a COP agreement. "Parties should, in all climate change related actions, fully respect human rights," read the agreement reached at COP16 in Cancun in 2010.[49] Second, in the domain of *human rights governance*, the strategy before the UN Human Rights Council consisted in returning to a focus on the broader linkage between human rights and the environment.

The institutional formula that unlocked the normative cascade on the environment and human rights was the Council's decision to appoint, in 2012, an Independent Expert tasked with compiling, analyzing, and clarifying human rights norms relating to the enjoyment of a right to a clean and healthy

---

March 10, 1995; Human Rights Commission Res. 1996/13, UN Doc. E/CN.4/RES/1996/13, April 19, 1996.

[46] Limon, Marc. 2022. "United Nations recognition of the universal right to a clean, healthy and sustainable environment: An eyewitness account." *Review of European, Comparative & International Environmental Law* 31 (2): 155–170; Limon, Marc. 2009. "Human Rights and Climate Change: Constructing a Case for Political Action." *Harvard Environmental Law Review* 33 (2): 439–476.

[47] Human Rights Council Res. 7/23, *supra* note 29.   [48] Human Rights Council, *supra* note 30.

[49] UNFCCC, Report of the Conference of the Parties on its sixteenth session, held in Cancun from 29 November to 10 December 2010, Part Two: Action taken by the Conference of the Parties at its sixteenth session, Pt. II.8, FCCC/CP/2010/7/Add.1, 15 March 2011.

environment.[50] The Council renewed the appointment of the Independent Expert (John Knox) for an additional three years and upgraded the mandate to a permanent Special Rapporteurship on human rights and the environment in 2015.

UN Special Rapporteurs (UNSRs) are textbook instances of norm entrepreneurship. In addition to conducting country missions, they produce thematic reports that clarify the state of international norms in their fields. In fragmented or emergent normative fields like the environment and human rights, they must strike a fine balance between norm clarification and norm creation. They need to track closely the existing level of interstate normative consensus, as they must report periodically to and seek the support of the Council and the international community of states at large. However, they also need to provide authoritative guidance on how to interpret and extend existing norms into new domains (like climate change) as well as suggest new norms that could fill the gaps that are common in global governance and international law regimes.

The story of this UN mandate was inextricably intertwined from the beginning with the idea of recognizing a new universal right to a healthy environment. Bearing in mind the successful effort of the UNSR on the right to water that led to the recognition by the UNGA of that right in 2010, state and civil society proponents of the Independent Expert (later Special Rapporteur) mandate on human rights and the environment hoped that it would play a similar role and achieve a similar result. The strategy paid off a decade later, with the 2021 UN Human Rights Council and the 2022 UNGA resolutions recognizing the universal right to a healthy environment.

The environment and human rights cascade is now coming full circle as it falls back down onto domestic law with renewed force. Several of the states that had not incorporated the right to a healthy environment into their legal system have recently done so. For instance, in 2023, Canada introduced substantial updates to its framework environmental law, the Canadian Environmental Protection Act. Among those changes is the explicit recognition of the right to a healthy environment and the government's duty to protect it.[51] Importantly for our purposes, the right to a healthy environment has become one of the core arguments in many domestic RCC lawsuits. And it has figured prominently in the hearings and state submissions leading to the advisory opinions on climate change by the IACtHR, the International Tribunal for the Law of the Sea (ITLOS), and the International Court of Justice (ICJ). Tellingly, one of the

---

[50] United Nations Human Rights Council, Draft Resolution on Human Rights and the Environment, UN Doc. A/HRC/19/L.8/Rev.1, March 20, 2012.

[51] Bill S-5, Strengthening Environmental Protection for a Healthier Canada Act, available at https://bit.ly/4cLiIVn.

four questions that ICJ justices asked during the December 2024 hearings on the matter in The Hague was precisely about the content and implications of the right to a healthy environment.[52]

In addition to the crafting of a new universal right, the UNSR and other norm entrepreneurs have been actively interpreting and expanding the reach of existing human rights to address the ecological emergencies of the Anthropocene. This is the process that former UNSR Knox has called the "greening of human rights."[53] I prefer to call it "climatizing human rights"[54] in order to home in on the ways in which human rights norms, rules, and institutions have been deployed in climate governance, including climate litigation. In investigating the linkage between climate and human rights, I also examine the extent to which a specific normative stream is emerging at the intersection of climate governance and human rights.

2.2.2 Climatizing Human Rights

This transnational process has proceeded in both directions of the climate–rights nexus. Advocates, litigants, courts, UN officials, and other norm entrepreneurs have climatized human rights by (1) assessing the impacts of global warming on the enjoyment of existing human rights and (2) articulating the need for climate policies to be consistent with human rights. The first direction entails assessing how current and future events induced by rising temperatures – for instance, heat waves, floods, wildfires, and hurricanes that are rendered more likely and more frequent by global warming – violate or create serious risks for the rights to life, physical integrity, health, food, water, housing, and other human rights. The opposite direction runs from human rights to climate change and hinges on the argument that effective climate action requires the respect, fulfillment, and protection of human rights. This entails, for instance, examining whether clean energy projects – from the extraction of minerals to the construction of massive facilities for renewable energy production – comply with substantive and procedural rights (e.g., Indigenous peoples' rights to free, prior and informed consultation and consent). As renewable energies expand rapidly around the world, the deployment of human rights norms to ensure a "just

---

[52] International Court of Justice. Public sitting held on Friday 13 December 2024, at 3 p.m., at the Peace Palace, President Salam presiding, on the Obligations of States in respect of Climate Change. December 13, 2024, available at: https://bit.ly/4aoURKA, at 40.

[53] Knox, *supra* note 27.

[54] Rodríguez-Garavito, César. 2023. "Climatizing Human Rights: Economic and Social Rights for the Anthropocene." In *The Oxford Handbook of Economic and Social Rights*, edited by Malcolm Langford and Katharine G. Young. Oxford Academic, from which the next two sections are largely drawn.

transition" has become an important concern for advocates and, increasingly, courts.

The UN OHCHR has, since the mid 2010s, actively promoted the articulation of the link between climate action and human rights. The decisive language of its 2015 report on the matter illustrates this turn. "Simply put," concluded the Commissioner, "climate change is a human rights problem and the human rights framework must be part of the solution."[55]

The OHCHR has not been alone in climatizing international human rights. As noted, the key norm entrepreneurs in this regard have been the UNSRs on human rights and the environment. Given the broad scope of their mandate, the UNSRs initially examined the environment–human rights connection in general, rather than the climate–rights nexus in particular.[56] The next UNSR, David Boyd, applied this analysis to climate change specifically. In his 2019 report on the matter, he went beyond legal doctrine and pointed to the policy consequences of reframing global warming as a human rights issue.[57]

The culmination of integrating climate change into the formal UN human rights architecture was the establishment of the UNSR on climate change and human rights in 2021. In its initial report to the UN General Assembly in 2022, the first UNSR, Ian Fry, foregrounded the debate on financial compensation for losses and damages incurred by vulnerable countries and communities due to global warming, which would come to dominate intergovernmental negotiations at COP27 in Egypt later that year.

To sum up, in terms of legal mobilization theory, both the advances and the shortcomings of the climatization of rights constitute central components of the legal opportunity structures (the "legal stock") that litigants, as well as some courts, are mobilizing in RCC cases.

2.2.3 Economic and Social Rights

A third normative stream feeding into the RCC litigation cascade has come from other quarters of human rights law and practice, especially economic and social rights. Lawsuits on rights like health, education, food, and housing exhibit several of the same traits as climate litigation in that they affect a large, geographically dispersed population, implicate numerous government agencies alleged to be responsible for pervasive policy failures that contribute to rights

---

[55] Office of the United Nations High Commissioner for Human Rights (OHCHR). 2015. "Understanding Human Rights and Climate Change," at 6. Available at: bit.ly/4cCY1Lb.

[56] Knox, John. 2018. "Report of the Special Rapporteur on the issue of human rights obligations relating to the enjoyment of a safe, clean, healthy and sustainable environment." A/HRC/37/59, Framework Principles 2, ¶4, January 24, 2018, available at: https://undocs.org/A/HRC/37/59.

[57] Boyd, ¶70, *supra* note 32.

violations, and tend to involve structural injunctive remedies and supervisory jurisdiction mechanisms to monitor compliance with courts' orders.[58]

The nature of economic and social rights also raises climate-relevant conceptual and legal issues that litigants and courts have been dealing with for several decades. While economic and social rights are justiciable legal norms, they are also programmatic statements meant to guide state and societal efforts at *progressively* attaining material well-being. Since governmental and societal duties associated with these rights are partially indeterminate, in that they can be fulfilled through a range of policy actions and are subject to resource availability, such duties cannot simply be complied with peremptorily. As noted, progressive realization and open-ended duties are also hallmarks of climate governance after Paris. This explains why RCC litigants and courts have drawn on economic and social rights norms in their submission and decisions.

The UN Committee on Economic, Social and Cultural Rights has contributed to fleshing out the climate–rights connection.[59] Its 2018 statement on climate change noted that state duties under the International Covenant on Economic, Social and Cultural Rights translated into obligations not only to adapt to but also to mitigate climate change. It also brought key principles of human rights law to bear on climate action by asserting that "a failure to prevent foreseeable human rights harm caused by climate change, or a failure to mobilize the maximum available resources in an effort to do so, could constitute a breach" of states' obligations to respect, fulfill, and protect human rights.[60]

In terms of the other direction of the rights–climate connection, the Committee has also highlighted the need for climate policies and programs to comply with human rights. For instance, in the 2019 joint statement on climate change that it issued with a number of human rights treaty bodies, it noted that in "the design and implementation of climate policies, States must also respect, protect and fulfil the rights of all, including by mandating human rights due diligence and ensuring access to education, awareness raising, environmental information and public participation in decision-making."[61]

The integration of climate governance and human rights has continued apace. However, as humans (and nonhumans) around the planet struggle to deal with or

---

[58] Rodríguez-Garavito, César. 2020. "Human Rights: The Global South's Route to Climate Litigation." *AJIL Unbound* 114: 40–44, from which this section is partially drawn.

[59] Center for International Environmental Law (CIEL) and The Global Initiative for Economic, Social and Cultural Rights GI-ESCR). 2020. "States' Human Rights Obligations in the Context of Climate Change." Available at: bit.ly/3WbPvM9.

[60] Committee on Economic, Social and Cultural Rights, Climate change and the International Covenant on Economic, Social and Cultural Rights, ¶6.

[61] UN Doc. HRI/2019/1, ¶7, September 16, 2019, available at: bit.ly/4fao4ej.

escape the highest temperatures the Earth has experienced in a million years,[62] the reality of the climate emergency has become painfully unavoidable. Since the legal stock of climate governance and human rights still falls short of what is needed to address those consequences, advocates have increasingly turned to courts to try to close the gap.

2.3 Riding the Wave: Human Rights Frames in Climate Litigation

The structure of legal opportunities is not the only relevant factor that influences advocates' decision to take an issue to court. Equally important are the subjective understandings of that issue and litigants' efforts to frame it in ways that resonate with courts and the larger public. This is evident in RCC legal actions, where the use of human rights language to frame climate harms as having a direct and individualized impact on basic human needs has been as relevant as the role of litigation in providing legal standards and institutional venues to advance those claims.

Indeed, reframing global warming in terms of its impacts on human individuals and communities was the central goal of the first-ever RCC case: the complaint filed by the Inuit people before the IACHR in 2005.[63] With the legal support of CIEL and Earthjustice, sixty-two Inuit based in Alaska and Canada asked the Commission to declare that, due to insufficient action on climate change and the promotion of fossil fuel extraction, the United States was responsible for human rights violations associated with the profound effects of global warming on the Inuit's Arctic homeland.

The Commission summarily dismissed the petition one year later. Nevertheless, the case had a long-lasting influence on the articulation of the rights-based mobilization frame that would come to characterize RCC writ large. As Marc Limon notes, the Inuit litigation "introduced the idea that rather than being a global and intangible phenomenon belonging squarely to the natural sciences, global climate change is in fact a very human process with demonstrable human cause and effect. It could thus, like any other aspect of human interaction, be placed within a human rights framework of responsibility, accountability, and justice."[64]

Although it would take another decade for RCC litigation to take off in earnest, the Inuit petition helped lay the foundation for the emerging norms and frames on climate and human rights. After the petition was filed, the

---

[62] Hansen, James, Sato, Makiko, and Ruedy, Reto. 2023. "The Climate Dice Are Loaded. Now, a New Frontier?" Available at: bit.ly/3W9K4xh.

[63] Jodoin, Sébastien and Corobow, Arielle. 2020. "Realizing the Right to Be Cold? Framing Processes and Outcomes Associated with the Inuit Petition on Human Rights and Global Warming." *Law and Society Review* 54 (1): 168–200.

[64] Limon, *supra* note 45.

Maldives government reached out to lawyers at CIEL to request advice on drafting a declaration on the matter. The result was the 2007 Malé Declaration, in which Small Island Developing States made the international human rights law case for urgent climate action and exhorted the UN Human Rights Council to take on the issue. This resulted in the aforementioned report of the OHCHR on climate change in 2009, as well as the first Human Rights Council resolution on the matter in 2008.[65]

The work of reframing climate change as a human rights issue involved a transnational advocacy network composed of a wide array of civil society organizations, state representatives, UN officials, funders, and other norm entrepreneurs. On the civil society side, the leading norm entrepreneurs were environmental organizations. They were involved not only in the foundational RCC cases but also in the broader efforts to formulate, disseminate, and internalize the international recognition of the right to a healthy environment and other norms at the intersection of environmental protection and human rights.

As someone who came to environmental law from a background in human rights, I remember feeling slightly out of place during the invite-only expert consultations convened by UNSR Knox early in his mandate to explore the connections between environmental law, climate change, and human rights. Over the course of two sweltering days in Panama in mid 2013, when we discussed normative standards for environmental defenders and other vulnerable groups, it became clear to me that the environment–rights nexus was a familiar topic of conversation for experts from environmental organizations, which made up the large majority of the group. The handful of us who initially came to this conversation from a human rights angle had missed the fruitful discussions taking place among environmental organizations since at least 2009, when the Friedrich Ebert Foundation sponsored an exploratory meeting on climate and human rights that was attended by environmental experts and policymakers, including former Prime Minister of Ireland Mary Robinson.[66] At a later UNSR expert consultation in Geneva in 2015, despite the welcoming atmosphere and the catch-up work that some of us had done in the interim, the impetus for mainstreaming climate and the environment as human rights issues in global governance was still coming from the environmental organizations in the room, including Earthjustice, Greenpeace, CIEL, and AIDA.

---

[65] Human Rights Council Res. 10/4, UN Doc. A/HRC/10/29, March 25, 2009.
[66] Interview with John Knox, former UNSR on human rights and the environment.

Interestingly, international human rights organizations such as Human Rights Watch (HRW) were conspicuously absent from or took a back seat in these formative years, as they resisted the expansion of the catalogue of rights and continued to focus on civil and political rights.[67] The contrasting views of human rights and environmental organizations were evident to the lawyers who sought to bridge the two fields through RCC litigation and other tactics. One of them was Peter Roderick, the environmental lawyer who, after working as a legal advisor to Friends of the Earth, co-founded with attorney Roda Verheyen the Climate Justice Programme in 2003 in order to use the law for climate justice. As he recounted in an interview for this study:

> [T]here's an environmental movement and there's a human rights movement and ne'er the two shall meet. There's always been this kind of artificial distinction. Although I tended to find that environmental people saw the human rights side of it quite easily and readily but not the other way around, and that's perhaps not surprising as well because environmentalists saw the power, if you like, the rhetorical and political power of human rights for environmental purposes, whereas human rights activists saw the environment not as about people but as about animals and plants.[68]

As this remark perceptively notes, environmental lawyers understood not only the *material* power of human rights – that is, the potential of mobilizing human rights law and institutions to pressure government and corporate actors to step up climate action – but also their *symbolic* power – that is, the potential of the rights frame as a narrative device that would put a human face to the climate emergency.

In retrospect, it is clear that the initial resistance of organizations like HRW to taking on environmental and climate issues was related to the broader debate within human rights circles about the desirability of expanding the catalogue of rights beyond civil and political rights. The domain where this debate most visibly played out was economic and social rights. Aryeh Neier, HRW's co-founder and former executive director, vocally opposed mixing socioeconomic justice and human rights causes. As late as 2013, Neier opined that taking on distributive justice issues would be "misunderstanding our mission" – apparently speaking not only of HRW but of the human rights movement at large.[69] Ken Roth, HRW's executive director for almost thirty years, famously wrote that many economic and social rights causes could not be productively tackled by HRW's "naming and

---

[67] Lock and Vanhala, *supra* note 25.
[68] Interview with Peter Roderick, co-founder of the Climate Justice Programme.
[69] Neier, Aryeh. 2013. "Misunderstanding Our Mission," Open Global Rights, July 23, 2013. Available at: www.openglobalrights.org/misunderstanding-our-mission/.

shaming" methodology, which required clarity about a violation, a violator, and a remedy.[70]

Elsewhere, I offer a critique of this view and its contrast with the dominant view among Global South human rights organizations.[71] Here I highlight two implications of HRW's and other INGOs' resistance to or slowness in addressing issues other than civil and political rights. First, it reveals the priority given to methodology over substance. The strategy of naming and shaming recalcitrant governments into compliance has been central to the success of many human rights efforts. But it blindsided some key organizations to issues that apparently did not fit neatly into it, such as socioeconomic injustice. Moreover, as the world changed rapidly and elected authoritarian leaders rose to power in countries around the world and proceeded to dismantle the rights and democratic rules that brought them to public office, naming and shaming became increasingly ineffective against populist leaders who are very keen to be named but are shameless, and who more often than not also resist climate action. Second, the reluctance to expand human rights' tactical toolkit helps explain not only HRW's but also other organizations' blind spot when it came to understanding climate change as a human rights issue. Indeed, climate change – with its nonlinear causality, planetary scale, and accelerating impacts – challenges the assumptions behind the conventional view of violation, victim, and remedy.

The disconnect was not lost on the environmental lawyers who puzzled at the cold reception they received when they approached human rights organizations to propose collaborations on the early RCC cases. As Roderick put it, those organizations questioned "whether environmental rights is a legitimate area for human rights. Many human rights activists don't like the idea of diluting – they see it as diluting human rights."[72]

Just as in the realm of economic and social rights, organizations like HRW that held a restrictive view of the range of human rights issues and methodologies were eventually outnumbered by those that came to see climate change as an existential threat to human rights. Albeit more than a decade after the Inuit petition, many of them, including Amnesty International and leading domestic NGOs, not only joined the effort to reframe climate governance in terms of human rights language but also became litigants or supporters of RCC cases.

---

[70] Roth, Kenneth. 2004. "Defending Economic, Social and Cultural Rights: Practical Issues Faced by an International Human Rights Organization." *Human Rights Quarterly* 26 (1): 63–73.

[71] Rodríguez-Garavito, César. 2021. "Human Rights 2030: Existential Challenges and a New Paradigm for the Human Rights Field." In *The Struggle for Human Rights: Essays in Honour of Philip Alston*, edited by Bhuta, Nehal et al. Oxford: Oxford University Press: 328–C22.N.

[72] Interview with Peter Roderick.

The catalytic moment was the lead-up to the Paris climate summit and the negotiation of a new global climate agreement, which provided opportunities for both environmental and human rights organizations to press the human rights frame. Although they aimed for human rights to be included in the operative provisions of the agreement, the ultimate reference to them in the preamble was nevertheless an acknowledgment of the climate–rights nexus. More importantly, the regulatory logic of the Paris Agreement created further opportunities for legal mobilization and domestic pressure on states to comply with and step up their mitigation targets and adaptation commitments. It is in the context of this hybrid climate–rights frame and structure of opportunities that litigation came to play a central role in the development of climate rights, as is evident in RCC lawsuits and rulings.

2.4 The Paris Regime and Rights-Based Climate Litigation

While the legal opportunities and frames of the global human rights regime have been crucial to RCC cases, developments in the climate regime have been equally as consequential to RCC litigation. In analyzing these developments, it is important to consider two core features of climate governance. First, climate change is not a single governance problem but rather consists of many regulatory issues. As Keohane and Victor argue, "climate change" is actually shorthand for several governance challenges: the coordination of emission regulation, the orchestration of common scientific assessments, financial compensation via emission control mechanisms like carbon markets or the Loss and Damage fund, and coordination of adaptation efforts.[73] Partly because of this, climate governance is characterized by a second trait: Rather than a hierarchically integrated regulatory system built around a single institution or normative framework, climate regulation is a "regime complex" – a loosely coupled set of institutional arrangements that govern narrower issues, from the production of authoritative scientific knowledge (through the IPCC) to states' mitigation and adaptation goals (through the UNFCCC and the Paris Agreement) to the financial regulation of loss and damage compensations and cross-border emissions trading, geo-engineering, and myriad other issues.

The climate regime complex has undergone two key processes that have been particularly impactful on RCC litigation: (1) the *normative* convergence around

---

[73] Keohane, Robert O. and Victor, David G. 2011. "The Regime Complex for Climate Change." *American Political Science Association* 9 (1): 7–23, 13. See also Sabel, Charles F. and Victor, David G. 2016. "Making the Paris Process More Effective: A New Approach to Policy Coordination on Global Climate Change." The Stanley Foundation, available at: bit.ly/3y1iLNG; Sabel, Charles F. and Victor, David G. 2022. *Fixing the Climate: Strategies for an Uncertain World*. Princeton: Princeton University Press.

the Paris Agreement and its implementation process and (2) the *scientific* consensus around the 2014, 2018, and 2021 IPCC reports, which articulated the human impacts of climate change with greater clarity and precision.[74] Studies on transnational environmental advocacy have documented how activists gradually complemented the dominant natural science-based frame with a human-centered frame after the failure of the negotiations that sought to extend the Kyoto model in Copenhagen in 2009.[75] A parallel human-centered turn took place in internationally authoritative scientific assessments, as evidence of the profound impacts of global warming on humans – including threats to habitats, health, food systems, economies, and political systems – grew rapidly.[76] The 2018 IPCC report has been especially influential in RCC litigation, as it offers explicit evidence on the need to keep global warming to 1.5°C (as opposed to 2°C) in order to save hundreds of millions of lives and to avoid other extreme effects on individuals and societies that are associated with that additional half-degree of global warming.[77]

In what follows, in analyzing the evolution of climate governance since the mid 2010s and its impact on RCC litigation, I include under the post-Paris climate regime both the normative convergence around the Paris Agreement and the scientific consensus around IPCC assessments.

2.4.1 The Logic and Setbacks of the Paris Model

The Paris Agreement's regulatory logic stands in contrast with the pre-Paris regime. In terms of Gráinne de Búrca, Robert Keohane, and Charles Sabel's typology of global governance, the climate regime went from an unsuccessful effort to establish a comprehensive, integrated regime (Kyoto) to an ongoing attempt to consolidate an experimentalist regime (Paris) that creates incentives for states to act on climate through an iterative process of international negotiations, domestic civil society pressure, emissions reporting based on IPCC methodologies, and periodic stocktaking and peer review of progress on climate mitigation and adaptation.[78]

---

[74] Intergovernmental Panel on Climate Change. 2014. *Climate Change 2014: Synthesis Report*. Geneva: IPCC; Intergovernmental Panel on Climate Change. 2018. *Global Warming of 1.5°C*. Geneva: IPCC; Intergovernmental Panel on Climate Change. 2021. *Climate Change 2021: The Physical Science Basis*. Geneva: IPCC.

[75] della Porta, Donatella and Parks, Louisa. 2014. "Framing Processes in the Climate Movement: From Climate Change to Climate Justice." In *Routledge Handbook of the Climate Change Movements*, edited by Matthias Dietz and Heiko Garrelts. New York: Routledge, at 19; Gach, Evan. 2019. "Normative Shifts in the Global Conception of Climate Change: The Growth of Climate Justice." *Social Sciences* 8 (1): 24.

[76] Wallace-Wells, *supra* note 16.   [77] IPCC, *Global Warming of 1.5°C*, *supra* note 73.

[78] de Búrca, Gráinne, Keohane, Robert O., Sabel, Charles F. 2014. "Global Experimentalist Governance." *British Journal of Political Science* 44: 477.

Regarding climate mitigation, it aims to limit "the increase in the global average temperature to well below 2°C above pre-industrial levels and pursuing efforts to limit the temperature increase to 1.5°C above pre-industrial levels."[79] As for adaptation, the Agreement aims to increase countries' adaptive capacity to the consequences of climate change already being felt. Through this, it aims to increase resilience and reduce the vulnerability of people to increasing and compounding climate impacts.[80]

In order to achieve the Agreement's goals, states are required to submit nationally determined contributions (NDCs) which detail the GHG emissions reduction and adaptation targets they set and the measures through which they will achieve those targets. Though states are required to submit these NDCs, their precise content and implementation are voluntary. Nevertheless, the NDCs are supposed to reflect each state's "highest possible ambition" and "represent a progression" in ambition over time.[81]

Iterative stocktaking processes – where states monitor progress in implementation of the Agreement – are intended to ensure governments act with the ambition and urgency needed to limit global warming and increasingly adapt to climate change. According to the regulatory logic of this model, these processes would create material and reputational incentives for states to articulate adequate commitments and subsequently implement them.

After the failure of the command-and-control model of the Kyoto Protocol, experimentalist scholars tended to view the Paris Agreement as a promising fresh start for climate governance.[82] The Agreement's reliance on decentralized and voluntary implementation of its key goals – crucially coupled with peer review and pressure to periodically ratchet up individual states' contributions – was seen as resembling the model of the Montreal Protocol that successfully dealt with the depletion of the ozone layer.

Given the Paris model's reliance on transparency and periodic ratcheting up of NDCs, it would succeed only if states have material and reputational incentives to deliver on their promises and to increase their ambition in order to reduce the considerable gap between the mitigation targets to which they committed in Paris and the emissions cuts that, according to the IPCC, are needed to keep global warming between 1.5°C and 2°C.[83] However, since those incentives are largely absent in the design and the subsequent implementation of the Paris model, states' NDCs have been grossly insufficient and there has been no real source of pressure for governments to ratchet them up as envisaged by

---

[79] Paris Agreement to the United Nations Framework Convention on Climate Change, Dec. 12, 2015, T.I.A.S. No. 16-1104, Art. 2(a).
[80] Ibid, Art. 2(b). [81] Ibid, Art. 4(3). [82] See, e.g., Sabel and Victor, *supra* note 72.
[83] Paris Agreement, *supra* note 78, Art. 4, para. 2.

the Paris Agreement. In practice, these gaps in the climate governance system were laid bare by the first five-year NDC stocktaking in Glasgow in 2021, where it became clear that virtually all governments had failed to implement even their plainly inadequate targets and that they had no plans to increase those targets to the levels recommended by science to avert climate catastrophe. While the agreements that resulted from the Glasgow COP failed to address these gaps, they did shorten the window for governments to propose new voluntary targets from five years to one year.[84]

With the Paris Agreement marking its tenth anniversary, the structural shortcomings of its regulatory model are now painfully clear. These shortcomings are laid bare by the collective failure of state parties to reach a trajectory that would avert dangerous scenarios of climate change: Under the current GHG emissions trajectory, the planet is on track to experience 3°C of warming this century.[85] Given that the central aim of the Paris Agreement is to limit warming to approximately 1.5°C, this gap between the current trajectory and the stated goal is evidence that the Paris model is in deep trouble. This conclusion is reinforced by the fact that "there has been negligible movement on NDCs since COP27," as UNEP concluded in its 2023 Emissions Gap Report.[86]

Climate negotiators who have been deeply invested in making Paris work acknowledge this model's failure, as of yet, to produce the material progress needed on emissions reductions and other climate goals. One legal advisor to vulnerable countries during COP negotiations concluded that, given the continued absence of sufficiently robust rules around transparency and accountability, parties to the Agreement have settled into a dysfunctional equilibrium that is, as it stands now, unable to deliver the needed ambition.[87] As 2024 came to a close – marked by the failure of COP29, the alarming news that it was the first year to exceed 1.5°C above pre-industrial temperatures, and the imminent withdrawal of the United States from the Paris Agreement – Elisa Morgera, the second UNSR on climate and human rights as well as an expert in international negotiations, assessed the status of the climate governance regime in refreshingly candid terms that evince the deep frustration of thoughtful insiders. "We can observe that some states are not acting in good faith in very clear ways, which is the basis of any international regime," she said. "There is widespread disregard for the rule of international law, and also a very clear pushback on the

---

[84] "All About the NDCs," United Nations. Available at: www.un.org/en/climatechange/all-about-ndcs; Glasgow Climate Pact, Decision -/CP.26, November 13, 2021. Available at: https://unfccc.int/documents/310475.
[85] Broken Record: Emissions Gap Report 2023, *supra* note 16.   [86] Ibid.
[87] Anonymized interview (ID#44).

science, and shrinking of civil spaces at all levels. Basically, the truth is out of the conversation. That is the problem – there is no space at COP for the truth."[88]

Looking back, from the outset, three structural features were incorporated into the Paris model in a bid to ensure that greater ambition materialized over time: (1) NDCs that would ratchet up over time; (2) an oversight mechanism comprised of rules and procedures that safeguarded transparency, including the Global Stocktake; and (3) climate finance. In the years following the adoption of the Agreement, state parties failed to articulate the concrete rules and procedures needed to fully operationalize each of these essential features, ultimately rendering the model ill-equipped to produce the transparency and accountability needed to secure sufficient ambition.

In particular, the evolution of the Global Stocktake illustrates how the model has entered into a state of stasis that is well off from where it needs to be to achieve the Agreement's stated aims. When the Agreement was adopted in 2015, there was substantial ambiguity as to how the model would be operationalized, including with respect to the Global Stocktake, which was envisioned as a process that would put pressure on states to ratchet up their emissions reductions through a transparent accounting of progress on mitigation. The dominant thinking, however, was that this ambiguity would be resolved through the implementation process.

That has failed to materialize; instead, the ambiguity has "metastasized," in the words of a seasoned COP negotiator.[89] With respect to the Global Stocktake, clear rules and procedures to ensure that the political realm takes into account technical information on the collective consistency of NDCs with the 1.5°C target have not yet materialized. As a result, the stocktake process has failed to serve as a source of pressure, as originally envisaged, for states to progressively increase their climate ambition. Combined with states' failure to pledge the needed levels of climate finance and meaningfully update their NDCs, this has produced an equilibrium wherein the international community is seriously off-track from the Paris temperature goal and yet has not yet grappled with how to get back on track.

2.4.2 Climate Litigation: Looking for Ways Forward in the Name of Paris

In retrospect, experimentalists' enthusiasm for the Paris model was partially unwarranted. As Sabel and Victor have acknowledged more recently, while

---

[88] Lakhani, Nina. "World's Climate Fight Needs Fundamental Reform, UN Expert Says: 'Some States Are Not Acting in Good Faith'." *The Guardian*, January 7, 2025, available at: https://bit.ly/40ikiZC.

[89] Anonymized interview (ID#44).

Paris moved away from Kyoto's ineffective top-down model, it did not evolve into the central node of the climate governance regime, as states failed to develop a collaborative process of experimentation with climate solutions as well as to increase ambition backed by credible penalties against noncooperative governments. Since "the opposite of a failure does not make a success,"[90] the Paris model has fallen considerably short of its promise to catalyze climate action. As anyone who attends the annual COP meetings can attest, climate summits have become largely ritualistic convenings whose value is measured more in terms of rhetorical statements than in effective commitments and actions to address the climate emergency.

To my mind, one of the reasons why insightful experimentalists missed some of the design flaws of the Paris model is experimentalist theory's relative inattention to the role of bottom-up pressure from non-state actors, from social movements to litigants to NGOs. For instance, while they rightly criticized Kyoto's top-down approach and understood the success of Paris as requiring a "two-level game" that also included pressure for compliance from below, they have largely focused on inter-state negotiations and paid limited attention to the role of the climate movement and climate litigation in exerting bottom-up pressure for states to increase their ambition and deliver on their promises on mitigation, adaptation, and loss and damage.

Elsewhere, I offer a critique of this blind spot and propose a variant of experimentalism that foregrounds bottom-up political and legal pressure for compliance in global governance regimes.[91] For the purposes of this Element, I argue that the majority of RCC suits and complaints (which focus on emissions cuts) can be understood as strategies to provide the Paris climate regime with procedural and substantive mechanisms that accelerate climate action by translating global mitigation targets into legally binding commitments at the domestic level.

Evidence from RCC cases suggests that litigants have leveraged this two-level structure of opportunities by (1) prompting courts to take the quantitative goals of the climate regime (as specified in the Paris Agreement and IPCC reports) as authoritative benchmarks to assess governments' climate action and (2) using the norms, frames, and enforcement tools of human rights to hold governments accountable to those benchmarks – and, increasingly, to go beyond Paris by acting with greater ambition and urgency when the Paris mechanisms and goals seem to be grossly insufficient to address human

---

[90] Sabel and Victor, *supra* note 72.
[91] Rodríguez-Garavito, César. 2005. "Global Governance and Labor Rights: Codes of Conduct and Anti-Sweatshop Struggles in Global Apparel Factories in Mexico and Guatemala." *Politics & Society* 33 (2): 203–333.

violations that particularly vulnerable communities are already experiencing. As Section 3 shows, this combination characterizes the large majority of RCC cases.

With the benefit of hindsight, experimentalist scholars have also come to the conclusion that the absence of penalties for noncompliance is a design flaw that has thwarted the efficacy of the Paris regime. Although not particularly enthusiastic about litigation, some of them have come to hold a view of the role of Paris that is similar to the one I see at play in many RCC lawsuits. According to Sabel and Victor, the UNFCCC consensus-based process of decision-making that frustrates advances on climate goals is also the source of legitimacy of Paris as the "climate conscience of the world."[92] Rather than taking place within the Paris legal architecture, climate action happens *in the name of* Paris through other institutional mechanisms, like litigation, that put the requisite pressure for compliance with climate goals on governments and corporations.

This view on the setbacks of Paris and the role of courts in helping to address them has been embraced by leading human rights tribunals. Indeed, the ECtHR, in its 2024 ruling on *Verein KlimaSeniorinnen* v. *Switzerland*, found that prioritizing climate protection over other considerations was justified, among other factors, by "the States' generally inadequate track record in taking action to address the risks of climate change that have become apparent in the past several decades."[93] In light of this, the Court tellingly concluded that "the question *is not whether, but how,* human rights courts should address the impacts of environmental harms on the enjoyment of human rights."[94]

The road leading to this conclusion was paved by more than 400 legal actions that reframed climate change as a human rights issue. The next section takes a deep dive into those cases as well as the actors and tactics behind them.

3 The Shape of the Field: Issues, Venues, Actors, and Strategies in Rights-Based Climate Litigation

Like any realm of legal practice, RCC litigation can be viewed from two different vantage points. From the internal perspective of litigants, judges, and other insiders, it consists of legal rules, procedures, and precedents. This viewpoint is preoccupied with the internal consistency of the norms and the technical issues of legal doctrine. In contrast, an observer looking at legal practice from the outside is mostly interested in the social context and the impact of litigation. From this external, socio-legal perspective, litigation can

---

[92] Sabel and Victor, *supra* note 72.
[93] *Verein KlimaSeniorinnen v. Switzerland*, 53600/20, Judgment, at ¶542 (European Court of Human Rights, Sept. 4, 2024).
[94] Ibid, ¶451 (emphasis added).

be understood as a social field where a diverse range of actors mobilize different forms of capital (be it organizational, economic, professional, or symbolic), sometimes collaborating and sometimes competing in the pursuit of social goals like climate action.[95]

While the previous sections combined both perspectives in documenting the trajectory of the field, this section adopts the external perspective by offering a socio-legal characterization of RCC litigation. The emphasis will be on describing the contours of the field as opposed to the details of legal doctrine. Section 4 will switch to the internal angle to dissect the doctrines and norms emerging from RCC litigation.

The section opens with a characterization of RCC cases. It examines the issues, parties, geographic distribution, and outcomes of the legal actions that were filed between 2005 and 2024. These and other variables (including the number that identifies each case) correspond to the information provided in the full list of cases (see Online Appendix). The section then takes a deep dive into the *who* of the field, from the pioneers of rights-based climate litigation through the entrance of a more diversified range of participants. Finally, the section turns to *how* the field operates, that is, the interactions, collaborations, and coalitions that actors have forged as RCC litigation has transitioned from an emergent to a consolidated field of practice.

3.1 The Shape of the Field

3.1.1 Evolution and Issues

Not long ago, documenting RCC cases was a relatively low-effort endeavor. As Figure 1 shows, in the mid 2010s, the number of lawsuits filed each year hovered around a dozen. As noted, the field became considerably more populated in the second half of the 2010s. As an increasing number of cases were filed in domestic, regional, and global jurisdictions, dedicated initiatives were needed to keep track of developments and trends in the field.

One such initiative is the original database that is used in this Element. Created by the NYU Climate Law Accelerator (CLX), it tracks all rights-based climate legal actions filed before judicial and quasi-judicial bodies.[96] The universe of cases includes a wide range of legal actions, including court challenges against governmental climate policy, petitions before domestic human rights commissions, litigation before the ECtHR, advisory opinion petitions before the ICJ and the IACtHR, and petitions filed before the UN

---

[95] Bourdieu, Peter. 1987. "The Force of Law: Toward a Sociology of the Juridical Field." *The Hastings Law Journal* 38: 805.

[96] See "Case Database," CLX Toolkit, available at https://bit.ly/40HFZUE. See Section 1 for an explanation of the sources and methodology of the database.

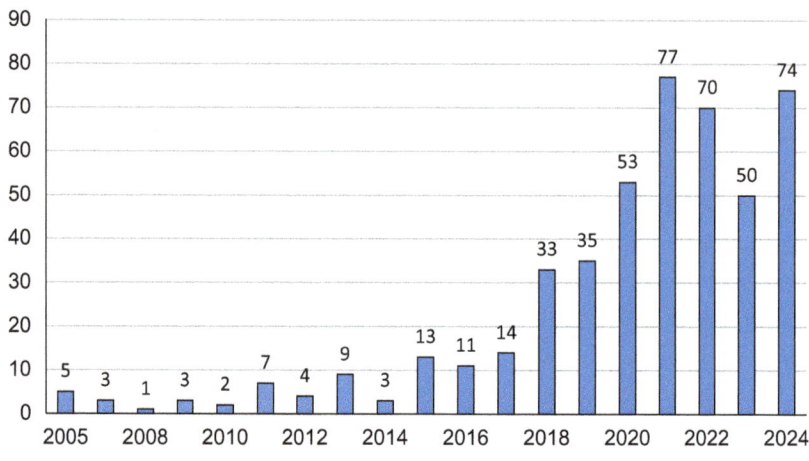

Figure 1 RCC cases filed since 2005.

Human Rights Committee and the UN Committee on the Rights of the Child.

Following standard practice in climate litigation research, the NYU CLX database counts a case as belonging to this ecosystem only if the petitioner or the judicial or quasi-judicial body explicitly mentions 'right' *and* 'climate change' in their submissions or decision.[97] This approach may exclude cases that, while not using that specific language, substantively revolve around issues of climate change and human rights. But it has the advantage of relying on a consistent, verifiable definition that avoids the pitfalls of leaving case count to analysts' subjective interpretation of the materials.

The first notable trend in the data is the proliferation of legal actions of this type after 2015. Indeed, the number of cases more than doubled every three years in the second half of the decade, peaking at seventy-seven in 2021. With the exception of 2023, the annual volume of litigation has remained near that peak.

What sort of disputes give rise to RCC litigation? A first approximation to this question consists in distinguishing between cases challenging climate policies and those challenging specific projects that deepen the climate emergency, such as oil, gas, and coal extraction. The majority (63 percent) of cases are complaints about *climate policies*. While some challenge the insufficient ambition of existing government policy (as in *Urgenda* and *Urgenda*-like cases), others demand that existing policies be enforced. The pioneering successful case of the latter sort is *Leghari* v. *Pakistan*, which the plaintiff filed in 2015 to challenge the government's failure to carry out provisions of the

---

[97] Peel, Jacqueline and Osofsky, Hari M. 2015. *Climate Change Litigation: Regulatory Pathways to Cleaner Energy*. Cambridge: Cambridge University Press, at 4–8.

country's climate law. Similarly, plaintiffs in the Brazilian *Climate Fund* case demanded that the government implement a law that had created a public fund for climate mitigation programs in the Amazon region, which the Bolsonaro administration had effectively frozen.

Moreover, a number of legal actions have challenged governments' failure to factor climate and human rights into environmental impact assessments (EIAs) when authorizing high-emission energy projects. For instance, in *Earthlife v. South Africa* and *Save Lamu v. Kenya*, environmental coalitions successfully sued their governments for omitting these impacts in EIAs that led to the authorization of coal-fired power plants.[98] In contrast, Canadian courts ruled in favor of the government in a similar challenge brought on behalf of youth plaintiffs against the expansion of a fossil fuel pipeline.[99]

Still, it is worth noting that 25 percent of RCC legal actions challenge specific *projects* that generate GHG emissions that, according to plaintiffs, are incongruent with the norms and goals of the human rights and climate governance regimes. These legal challenges seek to either block those projects or condition their execution to the fulfillment of substantive or procedural standards. For instance, in 2016, two Swedish NGOs were joined by 178 citizens in a lawsuit against their government for selling a state-owned coal-fired plant to a foreign firm with a poor climate record, which allegedly violated the government's duty of care and the plaintiffs' rights.[100] In a 2020 case filed before the East Africa Court of Justice, local and regional environmental organizations sought to overturn the Ugandan and Tanzanian governments' authorization of the East African Crude Oil Pipeline, alleging that the GHG emissions from this major project would violate human rights and environmental norms under national and international law. Similarly, in 2017, environmental organizations challenged the construction of a third runway in Vienna's airport for allegedly failing to adequately consider Austria's climate change and human rights commitments.[101] Other cases have targeted the approval of oil exploration projects in Argentina,[102] Guyana,[103] Norway,[104] and South Africa;[105] new coal mines in Australia;[106] a hydroelectric power dam in Chile;[107] liquified natural gas developments in Mozambique;[108] and biomass energy projects in Europe[109] and South Korea,[110] among others.

Another way of analyzing the focus of RCC cases is to classify them by the type of issue that they revolve around. As noted, climate change is not a single governance challenge but rather a bundle of distinct issues, including climate mitigation, adaptation, and compensation (loss and damage). These are the key substantive areas of the RCC field. Figure 2 represents their relative size.

---

[98] Cases 55 and 58. [99] Case 113. [100] Case 54. [101] Case 72. [102] Case 281.
[103] Case 202. [104] Cases 51 and 252. [105] Case 247. [106] Cases 147 and 167.
[107] Case 99. [108] Case 165. [109] Case 118. [110] Case 164.

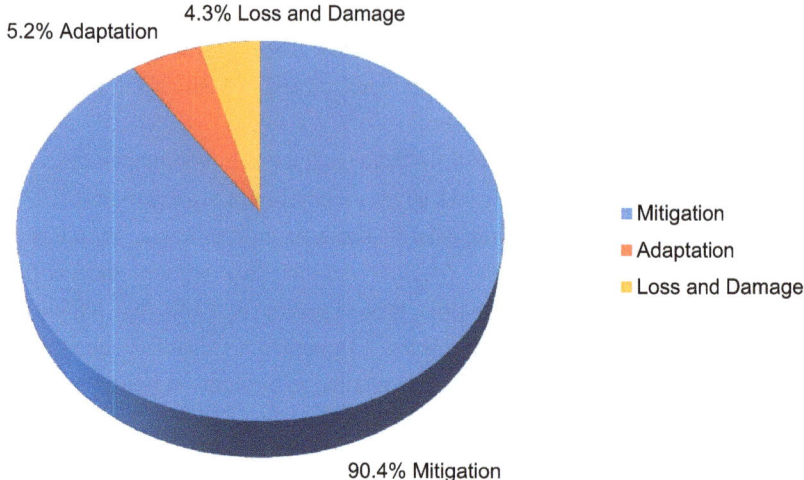

Figure 2 RCC cases by type of issue.

The predominance of mitigation cases is significant. On the one hand, the fact that nine out of ten legal actions seek to increase and accelerate GHG emissions cuts is unsurprising, as this is the key goal of climate governance. Given that emissions have continued to grow despite the 2015 Paris Agreement and the repeated and unequivocal alarms that the scientific community have sounded since, advocates have resorted to litigation as an emergency tool to prod governments (and to a lesser extent corporations) to decarbonize the world economy in time to avert the direst scenarios of a warming planet.

On the other hand, the dearth of cases on adaptation and loss and damage is puzzling in the face of the growing urgency and magnitude of these global challenges. Since it is too late to avoid dangerous levels of global warming, governments and communities around the world, especially in the most vulnerable countries of the Global South, have no option but to try to adapt to a hotter planet through measures such as putting in place defenses against floods or protecting people against extreme heat waves. Also, as the UN Secretary-General said before COP27 in Egypt, "we must also recognize that, in many places, it is too late for adaptation," which means that we need to urgently work on "closing the finance gap for addressing loss and damage" to fund rebuilding in vulnerable countries and communities affected by impacts for which there is no adaptation.[111]

---

[111] Mohammed, Amina J. 2022. "Secretary-General's Message on the Launch of the United Nations Environment Programme Adaptation Gap Report," United Nations, November 3, 2022. Available at: bit.ly/3LrG729.

Adaptation and compensation continue to be relative blind spots for RCC litigation, just as they are for climate governance writ large. The scarcity of cases on adaptation is particularly remarkable, as human rights norms and frames lend themselves more readily to adaptation than to mitigation lawsuits. Indeed, adaptation claims deal with localized impacts on concrete individuals and communities (as opposed to planetary impacts that affect all of humanity), which are the type of violations that human rights law is best suited to address.

Also, the adaptation and loss and damage blind spots in RCC litigation are striking because they are the most pressing issues for Global South countries, which have contributed the least to global warming and yet carry the heaviest adaptation and rebuilding burdens because of the disproportionate climate harms that they experience and the fewer resources they have at their disposal to deal with those harms.

As adaptation and loss and damage goals have become more salient at COPs and other climate governance venues, and as states and corporations have continued to fall short of their duties to adequately address and fund those goals, lawsuits focusing on these issues have experienced a slight increase. For instance, in *R v. Secretary of State for Environment, Food and Rural Affairs* a homeowner and disability rights activist challenged the United Kingdom's adaptation program for failing to protect them from heat waves and rising sea levels.[112] As for loss and damage, four Indonesian islanders sued the Swiss cement company Holcim, seeking compensation for damages they incurred from sea level rise on their island.[113] The islander plaintiffs also seek a reduction in Holcim's emissions and funds for adapting to climate change, as is common for loss and damage cases.

Finally, it is worth clarifying that not all RCC cases seek to further action against global warming. In fact, 11 percent of existing legal actions (fifty-two cases) *challenge* climate action. This figure includes four quite different types of lawsuits. First, corporations like Exxon have sued governments to oppose the latter's climate regulations or administrative decisions, alleging that they violate their right to property, free speech, and other corporate rights (twenty-two cases).[114] Second, in federalist countries, actions of this sort have been initiated by states against the federal government. In Canada, for instance, Alberta and Saskatchewan challenged the federal government's act that established carbon pricing, alleging that it overstepped federal authority because it concerned property rights and other matters of exclusive provincial concern (six cases).[115]

Third, some environmental and human rights organizations have challenged climate mitigation projects that, in their view, violate vulnerable communities'

---

[112] Case 361. [113] Case 296. [114] Cases 59, 100, and 317. [115] Cases 114 and 116.

rights (nine cases). For instance, legal actions have been initiated on behalf of the Indigenous Sami people in Norway and the Zapotec people in Mexico against the construction of wind farms in their territories, on the basis that government agencies and corporations involved in those projects violated the Indigenous communities' rights to culture and free, prior and informed consultation.[116] Cases of this sort seeking a *"just transition"* to a lower-carbon future are likely to proliferate as the construction of renewable energy facilities picks up.[117]

Fourth, as we will see in the next section, some governments and corporations have prosecuted protestors demanding climate action for allegedly impinging on other people's rights by blocking access to pipelines and pursuing other forms of direct action (sixteen cases).

3.1.2 Defendants

Figure 3 offers the breakdown of legal actions by type of target. The first notable finding is that, by far, the most common target are governments rather than corporations. This should not come as a surprise, as human rights law was developed historically to hold states accountable for human rights violations,

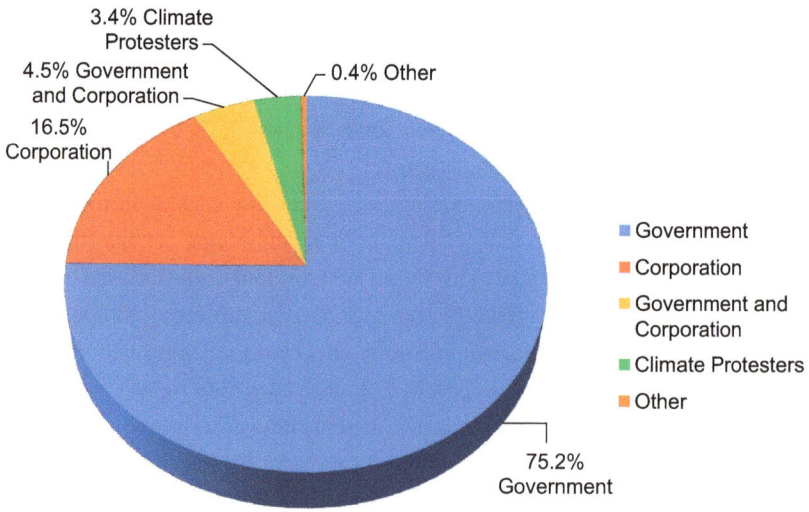

Figure 3 RCC cases by type of defendant

---

[116] Cases 94 and 162 respectively.
[117] Savaresi, Annalisa et al. 2023. "Just Transition: A New Knowledge Frontier." *Nature Sustainability.* Available at: bit.ly/4cJl7zR.

and the norms of the climate governance regime (including Paris) also primarily apply to governments. Also, this finding is congruent with the predominance of legal actions targeting policies as opposed to projects.

The breakdown of issues and defendants substantiates my argument about the role of RCC litigation in climate governance. In the face of the insufficient ambition and the enforcement failures of the global climate governance regime, the large majority of cases seek to exert material and symbolic pressure on governments to step up climate action in line with the Paris goals and the international scientific consensus as reflected in the IPCC's recommendations. To that end, the typical RCC case both leverages and pushes the boundaries of existing human rights norms by articulating legal doctrines that seek to adapt human rights law to the unique features of climate change as a governance challenge.

The other categories in Figure 3 are less predictable and point to noteworthy and even surprising developments. In previous work, I suggested that litigation against corporations was another blind spot of RCC litigation.[118] Until recently, only a handful of cases sought to hold corporations accountable for climate harms, despite the increasing availability of data on the historical emissions of the largest fossil fuel companies and the aggressive strategies that many of them have pursued to hide or deny climate science. This situation seems to be gradually changing, as a wide range of plaintiffs – from environmental and human rights organizations to city and state governments to public prosecutors – have launched legal actions against corporations to pressure them to align their business models with the goals of Paris and human rights law, deliver on and cease deceiving the public about their climate commitments, and compensate governments and communities for the impacts of the climate harms to which they have contributed. The result is that the proportion of rights-based litigation against only corporate defendants has almost doubled in the last two years.

The most frequent defendants are large private fossil fuel companies. In some cases, plaintiffs have sought to block energy companies' particularly carbon-intensive or environmentally destructive projects, such as Total's plans for a major oil project in Uganda and Tanzania,[119] or Shell's plans to conduct seismic testing off South Africa's Wild Coast.[120] In other cases, plaintiffs have launched broader challenges to corporate policies that, by expanding fossil fuel exploration and exploitation, run counter to the goals of Paris and the International Energy Agency's call to end the search for new oil and gas fields.[121] This is notably the case with respect to the complaint brought against

---

[118] Rodríguez-Garavito, *supra* note 19.   [119] Case 121.   [120] Case 247.
[121] "Net Zero by 2025: A Roadmap for the Global Energy Sector," International Energy Agency, October 2021. Available at: bit.ly/4cYMDcw.

Shell by Dutch environmental organizations including Milieudefensie (see Section 5).

Interestingly, recent legal actions go beyond challenging carbon majors in domestic jurisdictions. Some, like *ClientEarth* v. *Belgian National Bank* and *Conectas* v. *Brazilian National Economic and Social Development Bank*, have challenged banks that fund fossil fuel and other high-emitting companies. Others have targeted corporations in other sectors that have rarely figured into rights-based climate advocacy, despite their substantial contributions to the climate emergency. For instance, in 2021, environmental organizations from France, Brazil, and Colombia sued Casino (a French supermarket company) before a French court alleging that the company must take all necessary measures to exclude beef tied to deforestation and the grabbing of Indigenous territories from its supply chains in Brazil, Colombia, and elsewhere to comply with the French law on the corporate duty of vigilance. In addition to targeting corporate actors in the high-emission beef business, this lawsuit breaks new ground in trying to hold transnational companies accountable for the climate impacts associated with their supply chains.[122]

Although comprising a small fraction of RCC litigation, the sixteen cases involving criminal proceedings against protesters demanding climate action – wherein such protesters utilize rights in their defenses – should raise concern, especially considering the proliferation of new laws seeking to crack down on the right to protest against climate inaction in Europe and elsewhere.[123] For instance, the Canadian province of British Columbia brought charges against climate activists who had blocked access to state-owned oil pipeline terminals,[124] while the United Kingdom criminally prosecuted climate protestors for blocking a road in protest of the authorization of a fracking project.[125]

3.1.3 Plaintiffs

Classifying a case by type of plaintiff is not always straightforward, as many are initiated by dozens of actors of different sorts, from NGOs to youth collectives to individuals. Therefore, cases often fall under more than one category of plaintiff. For this reason, understanding the actors who pursue RCC litigation requires a more granular, qualitative approach that will be left for the second half of this section.

---

[122] Case 201.
[123] Lakhani, Nina, Gayle, Damien, and Taylor, Matthew. 2023. "How Criminalisation Is Being Used to Silence Climate Activists across the World," *The Guardian*, October 12, 2023. Available at: bit.ly/3Wdsl7Y.
[124] Case 80.   [125] Case 98.

It is worth noting that, other than individual adults, the most frequent types of plaintiffs are advocacy NGOs (43 percent of cases) and groups of young people (14 percent). While the role of NGOs is unsurprising, the frequent participation of young people as plaintiffs is a distinctive feature of RCC litigation that cuts across countries and regions. As we will see, the pioneer cases of this sort were filed in the United States and Uganda. However, the first court ruling finding in favor of youth plaintiffs was the Colombian Supreme Court's decision in the *Future Generations* case.[126] The Court ordered the government to deliver on its commitment to reduce deforestation in the Amazon, kept supervisory jurisdiction over the implementation of the case, and declared the Colombian Amazon as a subject of rights.

Youth involvement has infused the field with moral force and bottom-up political energy. And it has pressed human rights advocates and courts to take the issue of intergenerational justice seriously and adopt a forward-looking approach to remedies, which contrasts with the more familiar, backward-looking perspective of traditional human rights thought and practice.

3.1.4 Geographic Distribution: Regions and Countries

As the field has grown, its diversity has waxed and waned. In the mid 2010s, the Asia-Pacific region was handily the global headquarters of RCC litigation, with more than one-quarter (26 percent) of cases filed there by the end of 2015. Close on its heels was Latin America and the Caribbean, representing one in every five cases (20 percent) filed through the end of 2015. Before the turn of the decade, Europe and North America trailed behind the geographic frontrunners with 16 percent and 18 percent of cases, respectively. By 2021, however, the landscape had changed markedly. More than one-quarter of cases (26.4 percent) filed through the end of 2021 were filed in Europe, partly through the replication of *Urgenda*-like arguments in other jurisdictions,[127] with even more cases (27.5 percent) brought in Latin America. By the end of 2024, the field had consolidated yet further, with Europe (25.5 percent), Latin America (24 percent), and North America (22.5 percent) each competing for roughly a quarter of rights-based cases (see Figure 4). In the meantime, the sizable participation of the Asia-Pacific region has declined markedly, while regional and international cases have remained roughly the same.

Although Africa currently represents only 3.4 percent of RCC litigation, it played an important role in the rise of the field. Nigeria was the site of the first-ever RCC case that was filed before a court (as opposed to a quasi-judicial international human rights body). In mid 2005, Jonah Gbemre, a representative of the Niger Delta Iwherekan community, successfully sued Shell and the

---

[126] Case 74.   [127] Rodríguez-Garavito, *supra* note 19.

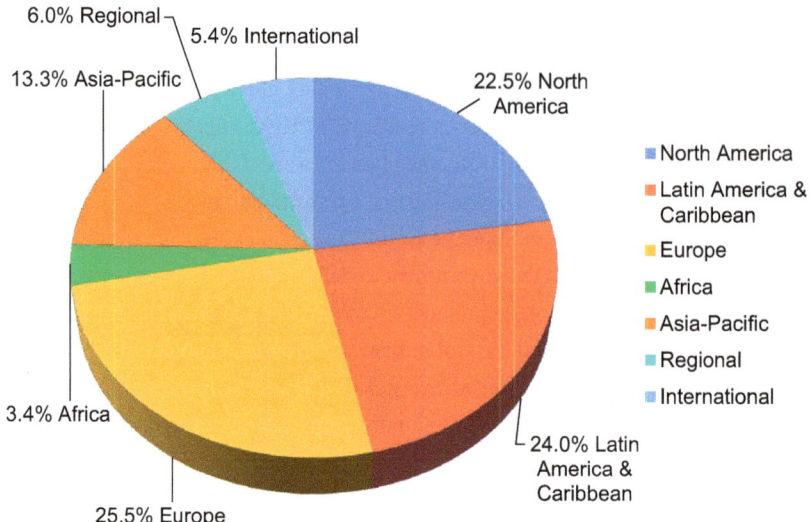

Figure 4 RCC cases by region.

Nigerian government for human rights violations stemming from the company's long-standing practice of gas flaring in the course of gas exploration and production.[128] While the lawsuit and the ruling of the Federal High Court of Nigeria centered on air pollution and its impacts on the rights to life, health, and the environment, they also referred to the negative climate impact of gas flaring. Moreover, in 2012, the Ugandan environmental organization Greenwatch filed the first-ever complaint focusing on climate adaptation in the Global South. Attorney Kenneth Kakuru, who would later become a judge, sued the Ugandan state for breaching its public trust and human rights duties by not taking the necessary measures to protect its citizens from floods and other climate impacts. The choice of young plaintiffs reflected the fact that the suit was developed in collaboration with OCT through the Environmental Law Alliance Worldwide.[129]

A more granular analysis of the data shows that the most active jurisdictions are the United States (ninety-four cases), Brazil (fifty-three cases), and Germany (thirty-three cases). Together, they represent roughly 38 percent of RCC litigation. It is worth delving in more detail into each of these countries, as

---

[128] Faturoti, Bukola, Agbaitoro, Godswill, Onya, Obinna. 2019. "Environmental Protection in the Nigerian Oil and Gas Industry and *Jonah Gbemre v. Shell PDC Nigeria Limited*: Let the Plunder Continue?" *African Journal of International and Comparative Law* 27 (2): 225–245; May, James R. and Dayo, Tiwajopelo. 2019. "Dignity and Environmental Justice in Nigeria: The Case of Gbemre v. Shell." *Widener Law Review* 25 (2): 267–284.

[129] Anonymized interview (ID #24).

the reasons for and the contours of rights-based climate litigation are somewhat different in each of them.

The United States is well known for its litigiousness, and climate change is not an exception to the country's tendency to judicialize major policy issues. However, US courts are also famously impervious to international human rights arguments, which makes the abundance of rights-based climate cases an empirical puzzle.[130] Two quite different reasons underlie this trend. First, one of the pioneer organizations in the ecosystem, OCT, has deployed a creative multi-year strategy that has entailed filing both a flagship federal case (*Juliana*) and similar cases at the state level. Since 2011, OCT has sued twelve states on behalf of youth plaintiffs seeking court declarations or injunctions against state governments' policies that, in promoting fossil fuel energy, violate young people's rights. Second, the proliferation of RCC litigation in the United States has been spurred by a trend pulling in the opposite direction: Energy companies and states have filed sixteen lawsuits *against* climate policies and initiatives. For instance, in 2016 Exxon sued the Massachusetts Attorney General Office arguing that the latter's investigation into the company's efforts to conceal the climate impact of GHG emissions violated Exxon's free speech and due process rights.[131]

In sum, the frequency of RCC cases in the United States stems from demand-side factors, that is, the dynamism of litigants requesting courts to intervene. As we will see in the analysis of the outcomes of the cases, the supply side of the field (that is, court willingness to step in) has gone in a different direction, as the conservative turn of US federal courts in recent decades and their reluctance to hear international human rights arguments have dampened RCC litigation.

This contrasts with the situation in Brazil and Germany, where both the demand for and the supply of judicial responses to the climate emergency underlie the relatively high number of cases. In both countries, human rights and environmental litigants benefit from favorable rules of standing, constitutional provisions on human rights and the environment, and judicial precedents that integrate international law into domestic law. In Brazil, an additional factor was the aggressive anti-environmentalism of the Bolsonaro government (2019–2022). Through a flurry of lawsuits, civil society organizations and political parties pushed back against policies that incentivized deforestation and rolled back climate goals, programs, and funding. Building on the Supreme Court's

---

[130] For example, Bayefsky, Anne and Fitzpatrick, Joan. 1992. "International Human Rights Law in United States Courts: A Comparative Perspective." *Michigan Journal of International Law* 14(1): 1–22.

[131] Case 59. See also Franta, Benjamin. 2021. "Early Oil Industry Disinformation on Climate Change." In *Environmental Politics* 30 (4): 663–668.

ruling in *Climate Fund* and the catalytic role of coalitions such as the Observatory for the Climate and funding organizations like the Institute for Climate and Society (ICS), rights-based climate lawsuits exploded from just six before 2019 to fifty-three by the end of 2024.[132]

Similarly, Germany went from having three cases before 2020 (the year *Neubauer* was filed) to thirty-three by late 2024. A whopping eighteen cases were filed in 2021 alone. That year, in the wake of the Constitutional Court's decision in *Neubauer*, youth plaintiffs supported by Deutsche Umwelthilfe (DUH; Environmental Action Germany) filed eleven separate lawsuits against ten German states for failing to pursue or implement ambitious climate mitigation policies. Similar to OCT's tactics in the United States, DUH and the youth plaintiffs alleged that German states' insufficient or nonexistent climate policies violated young people's fundamental rights and the states' duty to protect. Unlike in *Neubauer*, the Constitutional Court dismissed the eleven complaints, noting that the states were not violating the plaintiffs' rights because they are not bound by a carbon emissions budget like the federal government.[133]

In previous work, I suggested that Global South jurisdictions that exhibited a combination of favorable rules of standing, a dynamic community of public interest litigants, and a tradition of judicial activism on other issue areas (such as socioeconomic rights) would become prominent sites of RCC litigation.[134] This has turned out to be the case in countries ranging from Brazil to Mexico (eighteen cases), Argentina (twelve), Colombia (fourteen), and South Africa (nine). In a landmark case in Mexico, the Supreme Court struck down a government regulation increasing the permissible maximum ethanol fuel content, citing the potential for higher GHG emissions.[135] Subsequent complaints have challenged a range of energy policies and regulations that would have a similar effect.[136] In Colombia, litigants have challenged the authorization of fracking and coal mining projects, among others.[137] Argentinian courts have been less willing to intervene in the numerous RCC cases that have been

---

[132] See in general de Andrade Moreira, Danielle, Nina, Ana Lucia B, de Figueiredo Garrido, Carolina, Eduarda Segovia Barbosa Neves, Maria. 2024. "Rights-Based Climate Litigation in Brazil: An Assessment of Constitutional Cases before the Brazilian Supreme Court." *Journal of Human Rights Practice* 16(1): 47–70, available at: https://bit.ly/3C4txVy.

[133] Cases 227, 228, 232, 233, 234, 235, 236, 237, 238, 239, and 240. (An emissions budget refers to the finite quantity of carbon dioxide [CO_2] that can be emitted before reaching a limit on the increase in average temperature. See Section 4.)

[134] Rodríguez-Garavito, *supra* note 57. For an assessment of climate litigation in the Global South, see Lin, Jolene and Peel, Jacqueline. 2024. *Litigating Climate Change in the Global South*. Oxford: Oxford University Press. See also Tigre, Maria Antonia. "Climate Litigation in the Global South: Mapping Report." *Sabin Center for Climate Change Law*. June 2024. Available at: https://bit.ly/4jr254R.

[135] Case 119. [136] See, e.g., 127, 160, 177. [137] See, e.g., 159 and 378.

filed thus far, which have largely focused on challenging specific projects, such as offshore seismic exploration for oil.[138]

Until recently, South Africa and India were an exception to this trend. Despite their traditionally active litigation and jurisprudential traditions, and the key role of both countries in global climate governance, there were only a handful of cases in each jurisdiction, including *Earthlife* v. *South Africa* and *Pandey* v. *India*. Since 2021, the situation has changed in South Africa, where a spate of complaints has been filed. They include one of the few successful RCC lawsuits against a corporation, whereby a coalition of local communities and environmental organizations successfully challenged Shell's plans to conduct seismic testing off of South Africa's Wild Coast.[139] Meanwhile, the continued dearth of cases in India is symptomatic of the inhospitable context for public interest litigation and environmental advocacy under the increasingly autocratic rule of the Modi government.

In contrast, Pakistani litigants and courts have been active participants in the RCC ecosystem. The 2015 *Leghari* case set an early and significant international precedent in holding a government accountable for the failure to implement climate legislation. Mansoor Ali Shah, the judge who wrote the opinion of the Lahore High Court in *Leghari*, went on to become a Supreme Court justice, where he joined the majority in a constitutional complaint associated with the government's response to the massive floods of 2021.[140] Agreeing with the Court that citizens affected by the flood should be able to participate in the implementation of relief efforts, Shah underscored the existential threat that global warming poses for Pakistan and called on the government to step up its adaptation efforts.[141]

In the Global North, other than the United States and Germany, the most dynamic jurisdictions are the United Kingdom (eighteen cases), France (sixteen), Canada (twelve), Australia (eleven), New Zealand (nine), and the Netherlands (eight). Some of the most active litigants, both historically and currently, are located in the United Kingdom, including Plan B Earth, ClientEarth, and Friends of the Earth. For instance, in 2017 the environmental organization Plan B sued the UK government for failing to revise the country's 2050 carbon emissions reduction target in light of the Paris Agreement and the international scientific consensus on climate change.[142] One year later, it took another government agency to court for approving the expansion of the

---

[138] Cases 274, 281, 282, 371, and 372.
[139] Case 247. See, in general, Rodríguez-Garavito, César and Gallant, Jacqueline. 2023. "Addressing the Climate Emergency: The Untapped Potential of South African Constitutional Law." *Constitutional Court Review* 13: 125–145.
[140] Case 326.   [141] Ibid.   [142] Case 71.

Heathrow airport, alleging that it would result in a considerable increase in GHG emissions that would likely put even the insufficient 2050 target beyond reach and violate a range of human rights.[143]

France stands out as the jurisdiction with the highest percentage of cases targeting corporations. Upon closer inspection, about half of these cases have leveraged the legal opportunities offered by the 2017 law on corporate duty of vigilance to hold French corporations accountable for their contribution to climate change. Defendants include energy companies (Total and Electricité de France),[144] banks (BNP Paribas),[145] and supermarkets (Casino).[146] Other cases, notably *Notre Affair à Tous* v. *France*, have followed the more familiar strategy of suing the government to pressure it to take further action on climate change.[147]

In Canada, most complaints have followed the global trend, using RCC litigation to nudge federal and state governments to increase their mitigation efforts.[148] However, as we will see, a striking development is Canadian provinces' use of litigation to oppose federal climate action or prosecute climate protesters. In Australia, RCC litigation got off to a relatively late start with a successful challenge by the environmental group Youth Verdict against the Galilee Coal Project in 2020, based on Queensland's Human Rights Act.[149] As the Australian government adopted aggressive policies promoting coal extraction and resisted calls to reduce the country's large carbon footprint, other litigants filed complaints against coal mining projects and federal policy on behalf of youth activists, Indigenous peoples, and other plaintiffs.[150] Meanwhile, New Zealand stands out as the jurisdiction where the earliest and most well-known legal complaints were filed to recognize immigrants from a highly vulnerable country (Tuvalu) as climate refugees. Although ultimately unsuccessful, one of those claims (*Teitiota* v. *New Zealand*) led to a key decision by the Human Rights Committee which left the door open for future claims of this sort.[151]

Although less numerous than in other countries, cases from the Netherlands have had an outsize impact on the global RCC litigation ecosystem. This is largely due to pioneer challenges against the government (*Urgenda*) and a multinational energy company (*Milieudefensie* v. *Shell*), which set precedents that have inspired similar actions in other jurisdictions. Dutch litigants have skillfully exploited the opportunities offered by a legal system that integrates international and European human rights law into domestic law and have developed innovative legal strategies that integrate civil law and human rights

---

[143] Case 88. [144] Cases 121 and 162 respectively. [145] Case 346. [146] Case 201.
[147] Case 84. [148] Cases 88, 125, 130, and 145. [149] Case 147. [150] Case 167.
[151] Case 38.

law to address some of the most complex gaps of RCC litigation, from corporate responsibility for the extraction, burning, and funding of fossil fuel energy[152] to the extraterritorial impact of Dutch emissions.[153]

Finally, it is important to highlight the countries absent from these figures, particularly some of the world's highest GHG emitters. In fact, only seven of the top twenty emitters – the United States, Germany, Canada, Mexico, Brazil, Australia, and the United Kingdom – feature prominently. In other countries, the scope conditions for RCC litigation, including conducive legal opportunity structures and the availability of mobilizing frames and resources, are constrained by several factors. These include limitations to judicial independence in authoritarian regimes (e.g., China, Russia, Iran, Saudi Arabia, Vietnam) and illiberal governments (e.g., India), as well as stringent standing rules and a preference for nonjudicial conflict resolution mechanisms (e.g., Japan).

3.1.5 Regional and International Cases

During its twenty-year life, the field has become increasingly international. Partly due to the lack of familiarity with climate change as a human rights issue and partly due to deference given to domestic jurisdictions, international human rights bodies were initially reluctant to take on RCC cases. The Inuit case, the first climate complaint filed before a regional human rights entity, ended in a disappointingly elusive decision by the IACHR.

Given the slow and cautious pace of evolution of international law, the contrast with the situation only two decades later is striking.[154] In April 2024, the IACtHR held three multi-day massive public hearings on climate and human rights, with government representatives and hundreds of civil society advocates in attendance. The hearings were convened to gather information and views in preparation for the Court's advisory opinion on the matter, which was requested by the governments of Chile and Colombia. Just as it did in its landmark 2017 advisory opinion on human rights and the environment, the Court is likely to consolidate RCC law by clarifying and helping to settle the type of legal issues that the Commission seems to have felt were intractable at the time of the Inuit petition – from the framing of global warming as a human rights issue to the concrete climate action duties that governments have by virtue of their human rights commitments.

---

[152] Cases 122 and 173. [153] Case 366.
[154] For an analysis of regional and international cases, see Savaresi, Annalisa and Luporini, Ricardo. 2023. "International Human Rights Bodies and Climate Litigation: Don't Look Up?" *Review of European, Comparative & International Environmental Law* 32: 267–278.

Although regional and international RCC cases are predictably fewer (fifty-four) than domestic cases, their impact is likely to be deeper than their numbers suggest. For instance, the seven cases pending before the ECtHR at the time of writing as well as the favorable ruling in *Verein Klimaseniorinnen v. Switzerland* will have repercussions across a region that has inspired similar cases around the world.[155]

This global radiating effect has already been felt in the wake of decisions by the UN Human Rights Committee (UNHRC) and the UN Committee on the Rights of the Child. The UNHRC's 2018 General Comment on the right to life importantly recognized that "environmental degradation, climate change and unsustainable development constitute some of the most pressing and serious threats to the ability of present and future generations to enjoy the right to life."[156] In applying that doctrine to the two concrete cases that have been brought before it, the UNHRC has reached contrasting conclusions. *Teitiota v. New Zealand* entailed a complaint against New Zealand's denial of refugee status to a displaced individual who alleged that, because climate-induced sea level rise would make his native island country (Kiribati) uninhabitable, his right to life would be at risk if he returned. In 2020, the UNHRC found against the petitioner, arguing that, because Kiribati would not become uninhabitable for another ten to fifteen years, there was still time for the Kiribati government and the international community to take action to avoid that outcome. Rather than addressing the substantive issue at hand (life-threatening climate impacts that are likely to lead to massive forced displacement), the UNHRC opted to postpone it. Aware that this compromise solution could soon become insufficient in the face of growing climate-induced migration, the UNHRC importantly recognized that, in the future, receiving states like New Zealand would have the obligation to grant asylum to climate refugees.[157]

In contrast, in its second case on climate change, the UNHRC found in favor of the petitioners, a group of native inhabitants of the Torres Strait Islands who filed a complaint challenging the Australian government's dismal record on climate change, alleging that sea level rise and other climate impacts threatened their lives, livelihoods, and culture. Although (rather incongruously) concluding that the government had not violated the right to life of the petitioners (whose very survival is threatened by sea level rise), the Committee set a crucial

---

[155] Cases 252, 82, 294, 253, 258, 323, and 206. 2024. "Climate Change," European Court of Human Rights, April 2024. Available at: bit.ly/3Sf7nEV.

[156] Human Rights Committee 2018 General comment No. 36 (2018) on article 6 of the International Covenant on Civil and Political Rights, on the right to life, CCPR/C/GC/36, ¶62, October 30, 2018. Available at: bit.ly/3SczB2S.

[157] Case 38, Views adopted by the Committee, at ¶9.11.

precedent by framing climate change as a human rights issue and finding that Australia had violated the Indigenous petitioners' rights to culture as well as their right to private life, family, and home.[158]

In 2021, the UN Committee on the Rights of the Child issued its opinion on a complaint filed by sixteen children (including Greta Thunberg) from twelve different countries against five states (Argentina, Brazil, France, Germany, and Turkey) that are among the largest carbon emitters under the Committee's jurisdiction. Although it ultimately found that the complaints were inadmissible because the petitioners had failed to exhaust the available remedies in their domestic jurisdictions, the Committee crucially asserted states' extraterritorial responsibility for human rights violations stemming from global warming. Indeed, it concluded that states can be held accountable for violations suffered by children both inside and outside their territories, as long as those climate impacts are predictable and can be linked to states' actions or omissions.[159]

In a sign of consolidation of the field, the highest international tribunals dealing with human rights issues have been asked to intervene in RCC cases and clarify the law on the matter. For instance, in 2023, the UN General Assembly unanimously adopted a resolution seeking an advisory opinion from the ICJ on state obligations to address the widespread adverse impacts of climate change and related losses and damages to nature and people. Together with the IACtHR's opinion, the ICJ's pronouncement is likely to consolidate and lend international authority to some of the key RCC doctrines that have emerged from domestic jurisdictions over the last decade. Although human rights did not feature explicitly in the request for an advisory opinion to the ICJ, they were central to the arguments that many state delegations presented to the Court and were brought up in one of the four questions formulated by the justices during the December 2024 hearings.

3.1.6 Outcomes

This snapshot of RCC data leaves one key question: How are RCC cases being resolved? More than half of all RCC cases filed since 2005 (54 percent) remain pending or undecided (253 cases) (Figure 5).[160] This is unsurprising given the slow nature of litigation and that many of these cases were filed in the past few years. While most pending cases have yet to see a decision on the merits,[161] a number of these cases (17 percent) are being considered on appeal.

---

[158] Case 125. [159] Case 115.
[160] This includes cases where the court declined to dismiss the case and cases that are still being considered on appeal.
[161] This does not include cases where the court decided whether to issue a preliminary injunction before deciding on the merits.

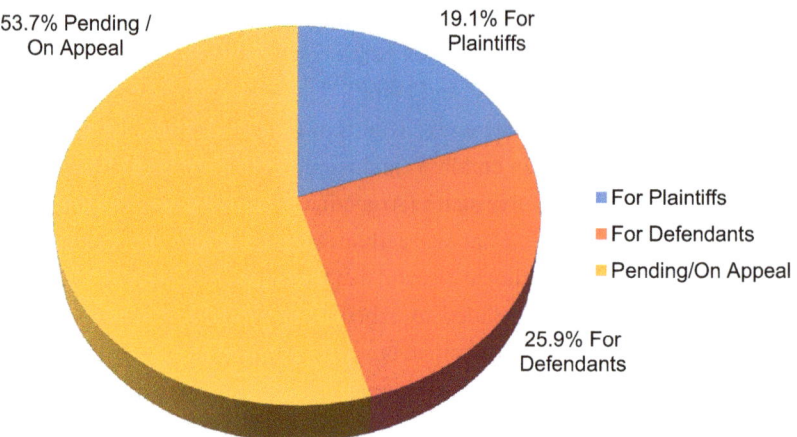

Figure 5 RCC cases by outcome.

When courts have reached the merits, they have sided with pro-climate action litigants in 46.6 percent of the cases that have reached a final resolution. Winning actors in these cases include plaintiffs in pro-climate cases and defendants in anti-climate or anti-climate protest cases. Governments and corporations resisting more ambitious climate action have prevailed in 53.3 percent of cases. They include defendants in pro-climate cases and plaintiffs in anti-climate or anti-climate protest cases.

Though results have been mixed, the fact that plaintiffs have won nearly half (ninety-eight) of finalized cases is striking, given the novelty and complexity of the factual and legal claims they have advanced. In doing so, pro-climate action litigants have made meaningful inroads in crafting an increasingly favorable body of jurisprudence for climate change and human rights

It generally takes longer for pro-climate plaintiffs to win a case than defendants. Cases are often dismissed in the early stages of litigation, and RCC plaintiffs may not have the resources to appeal the decision. In contrast, for a plaintiff to succeed they typically must progress through multiple stages of litigation and multiple appellate courts.

The case *VZW Klimaatzaak* v. *Belgium* illustrates this point. After the lawsuit was filed in 2015, the parties spent three years disputing whether the proceeding should be held in French, Dutch, or both. The court of first instance eventually ruled in part in favor of the plaintiffs in 2021, holding that the Belgian authorities had violated their duty of care and the plaintiffs' rights but declining to establish specific emissions reduction targets. In 2023, the court of appeal affirmed the lower court's finding of rights violations but went even further by setting a specific emissions reduction target for the Belgian authorities.¹⁶² The defendants, however, signaled their intent to appeal the decision, leaving the case formally undecided a decade after it was first initiated.

3.2 The RCC Field in Motion: Actors, Networks, and Collaborations

Now that we've seen the landscape of RCC cases, let's delve further into the actors behind this wave of litigation. Who are the actors driving rights-based climate litigation? And how do they operate and relate to each other? Based on evidence from interviews and participant observation, in what follows I round out the characterization of the field by offering a summary discussion of these questions.

3.2.1 Actors

Like any organizational ecosystem, RCC litigation includes different species of actors who serve and have served different functions. In keeping with ecological language, I distinguish five types of actors: ecosystem pioneers, disseminators, pollinators, supporters, and poly-culturalists. *Pioneers* were the first individuals and organizations to arrive on the scene, metabolizing the "rawest" of available materials to advance the earliest RCC cases and legal theories. This includes, among others, CIEL and Earthjustice, both of whom had lawyers involved in the Inuit petition. Their participation in this early landmark case is especially notable, given that both organizations also played a role in the convergence of human rights and environmental governance, demonstrated by their push, with others, for the inclusion of human rights language in the Paris Agreement.

Other ecosystem pioneers include the organizations that filed RCC lawsuits in the mid 2010s, including OCT (United States), Urgenda Foundation (Netherlands), Plan B (United Kingdom), Earthlife Africa (South Africa), Greenpeace (the Philippines and other countries), and Dejusticia (Colombia) as well as individuals like the lawyers behind the *Leghari* case in Pakistan. These actors were often professionally and personally connected, with ideas flowing between them in a series of organic as well as intentionally planned encounters.¹⁶³ As the lawyer Roda Verheyen has observed, for example, "every active lawyer in Europe taking on a climate case knows each other."¹⁶⁴ Similarly, an attorney who led climate cases on behalf of young people in the United States mentioned that her organization was in close contact and exchanged tactics with Greenwatch lawyers in Uganda, who went on to file a similar case in that country in 2012.¹⁶⁵

---

¹⁶² Case 40.   ¹⁶³ See, e.g., anonymized interview (ID#33); interview with Paul Crowley.
¹⁶⁴ Interview with Roda Verheyen, co-founder of the Climate Justice Programme.
¹⁶⁵ Anonymized interview (ID#24).

Some of the pioneer actors leveraged their global organizational structure to try out cases in multiple jurisdictions. This is notably the case of Greenpeace, which has filed and supported cases across a host of jurisdictions, including Indonesia, the Philippines, Norway, Germany, Austria, Luxembourg, Spain, Mexico, the Netherlands, Finland, Italy, and Argentina.[166]

Disseminators took the fertile openings created by their predecessors and expanded their range. In other words, these actors sought to replicate and add to the strategies of early RCC cases in other jurisdictions, adapting tested legal theories to the particularities of the jurisdiction.[167] For instance, the Climate Litigation Network played a notable role in facilitating the replication of the general theory of the *Urgenda* case in other European jurisdictions in particular.

Other organizations also actively sought to plant the seeds of early RCC cases in new jurisdictions. For example, Cordelia Bähr, one of the lawyers behind *Verein KlimaSeniorinnen v. Switzerland*, noted that "the inspiration was the *Urgenda* decision in the Netherlands. And I was asked by Greenpeace to find out whether we could do something similar in Switzerland as well."[168] Anne Julie Asselin, one of the attorneys behind *Environnmenet Jeunesse v. Canada*, echoed the inspiration of *Urgenda* while also pointing to the influence of the wave of children's rights cases filed in the United States.[169] Other lawyers, especially those located in the Global South, found inspiration in the *Leghari v. Pakistan* and the *Future Generations v. Colombia* rulings.[170] It is important to emphasize here that the flow of ideas between Global North and Global South jurisdictions have gone in both directions. For instance, Greenpeace translated into English the Colombian Supreme Court's ruling in the *Future Generations* case and attached it to their submission in the *Greenpeace Nordic Association v. Norway* case that challenged oil exploration in the Arctic.[171]

Field pollinators thread together an otherwise fragmented field, promoting the relational ties that enable denser and better-connected networks of practice and thus facilitating the consolidation of the field.[172] Pollinators have connected players in the field, offering spaces for dialogue and cross-jurisdictional learning and sharing. They have also provided databases and strategic research that

---

[166] Case 79; Case 42; Case 51; Case 87; Case 129; Case 144; Case 156; Cases 160, 188, 197; Case 173; Case 307; Case 325; Case 274.
[167] Interview with Paul Mougeolle, a researcher at Notre Affaire à Tous: "I think it's mainly replicating each other's work now, at least the main ideas."
[168] Interview with Cordelia Bähr, a lawyer at the Swiss law firm bähr ettwein.
[169] Interview with Anne Julie Asselin, a lawyer at the Québec law firm Trudel Johnston & Lespérance.
[170] Interview with Pooven Moodley, former Executive Director of Natural Justice Africa.
[171] Case 51.
[172] Hussein, Taz, Plummer, Matt and Breen, Bill. 2018. "How Field Catalysts Galvanize Social Change," *Stanford Social Innovation Review* 16 (1).

allow for the quick absorption of lessons from one jurisdiction to another. Such hubs include Columbia University's Sabin Center for Climate Change Law, LSE's Grantham Institute on Climate Change and the Environment, and the Latin American and Caribbean Climate Litigation Platform hosted by the Interamerican Association for Environmental Defense (AIDA).

In addition to producing research and facilitating connections, some actors in this category operate as litigation incubators. Catalyst hubs like NYU's Climate Law Accelerator (CLX) and Oxford's Climate Litigation Lab intentionally leverage the public goods they produce – from databases and case analyses to academic publications and training programs – to expedite cross-pollination among organizations and jurisdictions and support new cases.

Finally, *field supporters* have provided the field with the resources that have nurtured legal actions. There are two dominant sub-types of supporters: (1) funders and (2) scientific and technical experts.

Funders were few and far between in the early days of the ecosystem. As the rights framing of climate change became more popular and early cases served as proof of concept, funders increasingly stepped in. They included well-established, multipurpose philanthropies such as the Rockefeller Brothers Fund and Open Society Foundations as well as newer ones that were established specifically to support climate legal action, such as the Foundation for International Law for the Environment (FILE) and Brazil's ICS. In addition to financial support, funders like FILE and ICS operated as field catalysts by bringing together grantees and encouraging cross-learning and collaboration among them.

The increased availability of funding and connections helped provide the resources that were a precondition for the proliferation of this type of legal action.[173] This was evident, for instance, in the first convening of nearly fifty Brazilian climate litigation organizations, which took place in Rio de Janeiro in mid 2022. Organized and funded by ICS, the conference featured discussions of key national and international legal precedents, panels on climate science and policy, and strategic conversations about opportunities and priorities for future cases. Having participated in the much smaller and preliminary meetings on prospects for climate litigation in Brazil in 2016 and 2019, I was struck by the richness of the discussion in Rio and the number and diversity of participants. Only three years after the second of those meetings in São Paolo, participants from NGOs as well as academic and social movement circles spoke a common legal language that took a page from ongoing litigation in the country as well as leading cases in other jurisdictions. In a sign of organizational strength, many of the organizations in

---

[173] Interview with Eline Zeilmaker, Milieudefensie.

attendance had joined a nationwide climate-action coalition – the Observatory for the Climate (OC) – that has functioned as a domestic pollinator, as its key role in the *Climate Fund* case demonstrates. Although I collaborated with OC, ICS, and others to organize numerous online workshops on climate litigation for dozens of Brazilian organizations during the height of the pandemic, I could not have anticipated that they would go on to file nearly fifty RCC cases in the early 2020s, making Brazil the second most active jurisdiction in the field.

With respect to the second sub-type of supporting actors, from the earliest days of this litigation ecosystem, scientists and other experts have played a fundamental role. This is perhaps unsurprising as the success of most RCC cases is predicated on the availability of evidence that proves harm and links it to government or corporate actors. In practice, climate attribution science has been a key ingredient in RCC litigation.[174] But beyond the technical inputs provided as evidence, scientists and other experts have actively participated in the litigation design process, helping to shape the substance of the claims as well as the remedies requested based on the state of the best available science. Scientific partners in RCC litigation have ranged from individuals to organizations like the Union of Concerned Scientists (UCS).[175]

Finally, as the ecosystem of RCC litigation took on a more stable form, advancing from a handful of early cases to a global legal trend, organizations across an expanded range of themes and institutional niches – from civil rights and women's rights to Indigenous rights and rights of nature – have pursued their own RCC cases. These *poly-culturists* have taken the opportunities, lessons, and strategies offered by earlier RCC cases and embedded them in other related areas of rights-based legal action to pursue climate-related action. For instance, organizations working on corporate accountability have joined the field by filing RCC cases against banks that support GHG emission-intensive projects, as Conectas did by suing the Brazilian Bank for Economic and Social Development in 2022 and as Oxfam did in France in 2023 by co-filing a case against BNP Paribas.[176] With this widespread adoption, RCC litigation crossed the threshold of emergence and bears the markers of a stable, yet continually adapting, ecosystem of practice.

---

[174] Burger, Michael, Wentz, Jessica, and Metzger, Daniel J. 2022. "Climate Science and Human Rights." In Rodríguez-Garavito (ed.), *supra* note 19.

[175] Interview with Louise Fournier, Greenpeace International's Legal Unit; anonymized interview (ID#28).

[176] Cases 276 and 346, respectively.

3.2.2 Networks and Collaborations

Moving from actors to relations among them, I distinguish two key traits of the networks and collaborations that underlie the evolution of the RCC ecosystem: information sharing among actors and symbiotic relations between social movement organizations and litigators.

3.2.2.1 "Open-Source" Litigation Strategy

Interviews with key actors in the field as well as personal experience engaging with a variety of individuals and organizations working on RCC litigation make clear that, in general, an orientation toward collaboration as well as open lines of communication have become hallmarks of the litigation ecosystem. Compared to past waves of human rights and environmental legal action, RCC litigators and advocates have been particularly proactive in sharing their strategies and learning from others. For instance, Urgenda, Milieudefensie, and OCT have systematically documented and shared their strategies through dedicated websites.[177] Catalyst organizations like NYU's Climate Law Accelerator and AIDA's Latin American platform have expanded collaboration and cross-learning through case studies, toolkits, and online events that digest strategic learnings from existing lawsuits and facilitate their adoption in new cases.[178] In the words of an attorney with Global Legal Action Network, which filed the *Duarte Agostino* v. *Portugal* case, "our approach from the outset was very much to share our thinking as far and wide as possible."[179] This approach, which can be called *open-source litigation*, has encouraged replication and creative adaptation in the RCC field.

On the flip side, litigators and advocates seeking to bring their own cases, especially in the earlier days of the ecosystem, have sought out the advice of those involved in precedent-setting cases, who have often been largely responsive to requests for strategic insight.[180] This collaborative approach also extends to interdisciplinary encounters, as litigators have sought the counsel of scientists. Scientist collectives such as UCS have gone as far as establishing programs to support climate litigation. According to Delta Merner, a lead scientist in the Science Hub for Climate Litigation at UCS, there is increasing

---

[177] "Landmark Decision by Dutch Supreme Court," Urgenda. Available at: www.urgenda.nl/en/themas/climate-case/; Our Children's Trust. Available at: www.ourchildrenstrust.org/; "Our Climate Case Against Shell," Milieudefensie. Available at: https://en.milieudefensie.nl/climate-case-shell/our-climate-case-against-shell.

[178] "CLX Toolkit," *supra* note 20; "Plataforma de Litigio Climático para América Latina y el Caribe," AIDA. Available at: https://litigioclimatico.com/es.

[179] Anonymized interview (#17).

[180] See, e.g., interview with Sjoukje Van Oosterhout, Milieudefensie.

demand for litigation-relevant science: "litigators want to hear the science voice. They want to understand it. They want to ask questions."[181] Interestingly, scientists have not always approached participation in litigation with the same openness, in part the result of a hesitance to engage in activities that could create the perception of professional bias. This reticence is one that organizations like UCS have sought to counter, working to normalize scientists' participation in litigation much like the scientific community's participation in other realms of the legal system, like forensic analysis.[182]

Although there are exceptions to this trait, where limited availability of funding encourages proprietary approaches, the conclusion of Michelle Jonker-Argueta, Senior Legal Counsel with Greenpeace International's Legal Unit, is representative of views in the field. "Lawyers pushing for climate justice through the courts around the world, we talk – we exchange ideas, talk about legal theories," she said. "We find inspiration in what other people are doing and have done."[183]

The forces driving the adoption of this ethos are varied and difficult to fully disentangle. Two potential drivers, however, are worth noting. First, there is widespread recognition of the existential urgency of climate change as well as the fact that addressing it requires global action, which means that for RCC litigation to be truly effective, it must be pursued simultaneously in multiple countries and venues.[184] As one litigator put it, "we have to try and besiege the Citadel."[185] As Anne Julie Asselin added: "what's good is that it's coming from everywhere from every country … it's such a global issue that we need courts from everywhere around the globe to say the same thing to governments."[186] The urgency and necessity of widespread action encourages an open-source, collaborative approach. Second, the individuals and organizations that initially built out the ecosystem were not, in general, flagship human rights organizations. That pioneers of the RCC litigation ecosystem were smaller, more resource-constrained, and typically (though not always) less established may have lent itself to greater flexibility and less institutional ownership in encounters with others.[187]

Finally, the emphasis on information sharing accelerated the cross-jurisdictional uptake of legal theories, strategies, and lessons as well as laid the groundwork for collaboration. In terms of information sharing, there are two defining features: information aggregation and channels of communication.

---

[181] Interview with Delta Merner, Union of Concerned Scientists. [182] Ibid.
[183] Interview with Michelle Jonker-Argueta, Greenpeace International.
[184] See, e.g., anonymized interview (ID#6).
[185] Interview with Gerry Liston, Global Legal Action Network (GLAN).
[186] Interview with Anne Julie Asselin. [187] See, e.g., anonymized interview (ID#14).

With respect to information aggregation, databases that collect and make sense of climate cases around the world have been essential components of the global spread of this type of legal action.[188] Perhaps most significant of these databases have been the Climate Change Litigation Databases maintained by Columbia University's Sabin Center for Climate Change Law.[189] Also of note is the Climate Change Laws of the World database supplied by LSE's Grantham Institute as well as the rights-based climate case chart and toolkit maintained by the NYU Climate Law Accelerator. In terms of information production and distillation, nonlegal researchers have also played a key role, compiling field-relevant tools like the Climate Action Tracker, which assesses country compliance with the Paris Agreement.[190]

Various ecosystem-specific information channels have facilitated the exchange of ideas, updates, and insights. These channels include the Climate Law listserv as well as *The Wave*, a specialized, independent journalistic outlet that covers developments in the climate litigation field. Training programs for litigators and transnational exchanges among judges have served as important channels to inform key players of developments in jurisprudence and relevant scientific evidence. In the words of a Ugandan climate lawyer, while in the past judges "would just dismiss them [for] only technicalities or lack of cause of action ... now because of ... the climate justice trainings, and some of the judges have gone through it, there is realization that when these matters come to the courts, they should be given the attention that they deserve."[191]

3.2.2.2 Symbiosis: Social and Political Mobilization in Rights-Based Climate Litigation

When compared with other forms of rights-based legal mobilization, one of the most striking features of RCC litigation is the leading role of social movement organizations as opposed to specialized law-oriented organizations. Interestingly, this has been the silver lining of well-established human rights organizations' initial reluctance to frame global warming as a human rights issue and pursue legal action to hold governments and corporations accountable for climate-induced human rights violations.

While the excessive reliance on legal discourse has been an obstacle to innovation and cross-movement collaboration in other human rights sub-fields,[192]

---

[188] See, e.g., interview with Mark Odaga, Natural Justice Africa.
[189] See, e.g., interview with Maria Antonia Tigre, Columbia Sabin Center for Climate Change Law.
[190] Climate Action Tracker. Available at: https://climateactiontracker.org/.
[191] Anonymized interview (ID#22).
[192] Sen, Amartya. 2006. "Human Rights and the Limits of the Law." *Cardozo Law Review* 27 (6): 2913–2926.

the heavy involvement of environmental organizations and collectives in RCC litigation helps explain why, in many of the landmark cases, legal action is embedded in a broader mobilization strategy that includes protests, transnational campaigns, and plaintiff-centered communication tactics. Instead of the largest international and domestic law-oriented organizations, often it has been the smaller movement organizations that have led the way. As a British climate lawyer put it, "partly because *Urgenda* was such an influence and OCT were such influences and looking at Mr. Leghari, the farmer in Pakistan, and thinking these aren't the giant NGOs bringing this action. These are smaller, citizen, grassroots-type enterprises."[193] Indeed, it is not uncommon for RCC lawsuits to be filed by dozens and even hundreds of petitioners and for the latter to be the public faces of the cases.[194] For instance, the 2015 *VZW Klimaatzaak* v. *Belgium* lawsuit was filed by 58,000 co-plaintiffs who requested that the federal and regional governments reduce GHG emissions based on the rights to life and private life as well as the principle of intergenerational justice.[195]

Just like in natural ecosystems, symbiotic relations between grassroots and litigation organizations have facilitated the growth of the RCC ecosystem. Sometimes, those symbiotic relationships have emerged within a single organization. Greenpeace, a global advocacy organization, has been an important player in the field thanks to the close collaboration between its well-established campaign and communications teams with its newer Climate Justice & Liability unit.[196]

The centrality of political and legal mobilization is evident in the repertoire of tactics that is typical of RCC lawsuits. At key moments of litigation proceedings, like the filing of a case or a court hearing, advocates oftentimes organize online petitions, direct actions, and media blitzes in support of the case.

Collaborations between climate lawyers and the youth climate movement are a particularly telling example. Litigators and others in the RCC ecosystem have pointed time and again to the surge in climate activism that began in the mid 2010s and was turbocharged with the rise of the youth climate movement, especially the launch of the school strikes; for many, decisions to file RCC cases or choice of plaintiff – especially youth – were influenced by the cultural salience of street mobilizations around climate change.[197] Some litigators

---

[193] Anonymized interview (ID#6).   [194] See, e.g., Case 148, Case 74, and Case 29.
[195] Case 40.
[196] See Casper, Kristin, Fournier, Louise, Harvey, Richard, Jonker-Argueta, Michelle, Valente, Kasey, and Sharma, Amrekha. 2024. "Breaking the Mould in the Strategic Design and Implementation of Climate Litigation." In *Research Handbook on Climate Change Litigation*, edited by Sindico, Franceso, McKenzie, Kate, A Medici-Colombo, Gastón, and Wegener, Lennart. Cheltenham: Edward Elgar: 37–56, accessed January 21, 2025, available at: https://bit.ly/40KUJ5e.
[197] See, e.g., interview with Sjoukje Van Oosterhout.

explicitly sought to translate the power and moral clarity of the youth movement into legal wins. For the team behind *Environnement Jeunesse* v. *Canada*, the goal was "to share the youth voice that young people are very serious about the climate crisis."[198]

This has been a two-way street: Youth activists have also sought out lawyers to help them amplify the impact of the youth movement through RCC litigation. The German youth activist Luisa Neubauer, for example, proactively contacted a German lawyer to inquire on the possibility of filing a youth-led case that challenged the inadequacies of a recently passed climate law.

> I've learned that in some other countries, they had sued the governments, [so] I called this lawyer [Roda Verheyen] and said 'hello, I'm Louisa from the Fridays [for Future], can we do something about this?' And she was like 'ehhh' ... and four months later she came back and she said we can do something and we're going to do it with 10–20 other youth people, different NGOs, [and] we're going to do it as collective case in front of the Constitutional Court.[199]

Hence, the youth climate activist's proactive outreach helped prompt the filing of the *Neubauer* v. *Germany* case.

Press and media coverage have facilitated symbiosis between RCC litigation and the wider climate movement, amplifying the voices and perspectives litigators have later sought to translate into legal action while also spotlighting litigation as a tool to advance certain movement goals. As Chima Williams, a Nigerian lawyer with experience in climate litigation, said, "no matter what we do, if we stay within the four walls of the court and use all our legal language, if the media is not involved to send the message outside of the four walls, then it will amount to us speaking to ourselves. The media is a strategic ally for us in this suit."[200]

Litigators and advocates involved in RCC litigation often have made intensive efforts to cultivate relationships with journalists, educate them on the facts and circumstances of the case, and otherwise raise the profile of the litigation in the media through interviews, press conferences, and the like. In the words of Sjoukje Van Oosterhout, one of the Milieudefensie advocates involved in the legal action against Shell, "our press team deserves a lot of credit for building media relations over the last years. I think a big part of our strategy there was also providing a lot of knowledge to the journalists."[201] The ultimate aim of this

---

[198] Interview with Catherine Gauthier, Environnement Jeunesse.
[199] Panel x ChangeNOW. 2023. "Civic Action: From Awareness to Movements (Interview with Luisa Neubauer)." May 27, 2023. Available at: bit.ly/4fnoUVp (YouTube transcript used).
[200] Interview with Chima Williams, Environmental Rights Action (Nigeria).
[201] See interview with Sjoukje Van Oosterhout.

has been to increase the salience and resonance of the case and the issues raised therein with the public, with an eye toward stimulating mobilization around the case and climate change more generally.[202]

As we have seen in this section, over the course of the past twenty years, rights-based climate litigation has transformed from a novel idea with limited traction to a widespread legal phenomenon comprising hundreds of cases across six continents. This trend is best understood from multiple angles, from types of defendants and plaintiffs to choice of target to outcome. Beyond the *what* of RCC litigation, this section also delved into the *who*: the various actors that make up this litigation ecosystem and the patterns of collaboration and communication between them that have facilitated the relatively rapid proliferation of this form of legal practice. We will now move from this external point of view – the socio-legal assessment of the field, its actors, and its modes of operating – to an internal point of view in the next section, which will delve into the legal rules, procedures, and precedents – the doctrinal and jurisprudential standards, broadly speaking – of RCC litigation.

4 Addressing the Unique Challenges of Global Warming: The Evolving Law of Human Rights and Climate Change

On April 9, 2024, the Grand Chamber of the ECtHR handed down a landmark ruling in a case against Switzerland that had been filed eight years earlier by the association Swiss Senior Women for Climate Protection. The ECtHR held that the Swiss government's policies had fallen considerably short of the ambition and urgency recommended by the IPCC and the Paris framework and thus violated the rights of the plaintiffs, who are part of a population that is disproportionately affected by the heat waves that have become more frequent and extreme due to global warming.

What is particularly revealing about the ruling is its categorical conclusion on the connection between human rights, environmental protection, and climate action as a matter of law. According to the Court, "the question is no longer whether, but how, human rights courts should address the impacts of environmental harms on the enjoyment of human rights."[203] This stands in the starkest contrast with the conclusion of the IACHR in the Inuit case. In its cryptic letter to the petitioners in 2006, the Commission concluded that "the information

---

[202] See, e.g., anonymized interview (ID#24).
[203] Case 52 (*Verein KlimaSeniorinnen v. Switzerland*, 53600/20, Judgment at ¶451 (European Court of Human Rights, Sept. 4, 2024)).

provided does not enable us to determine whether the alleged facts would tend to characterize a violation of rights protected by the American Declaration."[204]

This contrast is particularly telling because the Inter-American System has tended to be more expansive than the ECtHR in the protection of human rights harms stemming from environmental degradation. Rather than a symptom of different views on climate change, the disparity is a signal of the deep and relatively rapid transformation of legal doctrine and jurisprudence over the last two decades. Indeed, it is very likely that the Inter-American Commission would reach a different conclusion if the Inuit petition were filed today. Rather than breaking new legal ground, the ECtHR's decision followed the increasingly converging views of domestic courts and UN treaty bodies on climate change as a human rights issue.

In this section, I sketch the contours of the norms that constitute this broad legal convergence as well as the areas of ongoing jurisprudential contention. This section's perspective is that of the insiders to legal practice, who focus on articulating the applicable norms, formulating legal arguments, and offering interpretations of relevant sources. This internal point of view helps us distill the normative content of the RCC field – the principles and rules that litigators and courts have developed to address climate harms. This "legal stock" serves as the basis for future legal actions, thus feeding an iterative transnational process whereby RCC litigation effectively contributes to shaping climate governance.

To make this rapidly growing body of law tractable, this section is organized according to a short list of key questions that courts and quasi-judicial entities have sought to answer. It begins with a preliminary question: Is climate change a justiciable human rights issue? I unpack this question by examining how adjudicators have framed global warming as a human rights topic, affirmed their power to review climate policy, and identified the relevant body of norms by integrating standards from human rights and climate law.

Thereafter, I discuss the doctrines that address the overarching substantive question of RCC litigation: In a given case, are government and corporate actions around climate change compatible with their human rights duties and responsibilities? This generic question, in turn, entails a set of questions and doctrinal issues tied to the unique nature of climate change and which are very much alive in the global practice of rights-based litigation: Who has standing to sue? What are the rights-based duties of individual states or corporations? How do those duties change over time as the climate emergency accelerates and

---

[204] Case 1 (*Petition to the IACHR Seeking Relief from Violations Resulting from Global Warming Caused by Acts and Omissions of the United States*, Letter of Dismissal at 1 (Inter-American Commission on Human Rights, Nov. 16, 2006)).

becomes entrenched? Are defendants accountable for climate harms beyond their jurisdiction?

Before proceeding, a note on the level of granularity of the answers to these questions is in order. For the sake of clarity and brevity, the section omits some legal intricacies that are relevant to judges, litigators, and other practitioners. Although this section does delve into the details of doctrine, I do without long quotes from relevant decisions and have likewise omitted in-depth technical discussions. Those interested in greater detail can find extended discussions of the relevant cases and doctrines in the companion website that also contains the Element's underlying database.[205]

4.1 Is Climate Change a Justiciable Human Rights Issue?

4.1.1 Climate Change Is a Matter of Human Rights

Beginning in the mid 2010s, pioneering decisions began to affirm what is now the prevailing view: Climate impacts can generate cognizable human rights violations, and governments and other actors can be held legally accountable for such violations. One of the earliest decisions to conclusively link climate change to human rights impacts, including the potential for justiciable rights violations, was *Leghari v. Pakistan*. In *Leghari*, a Pakistani farmer argued that the government's failure to implement its climate change legislation generated impacts that infringed on fundamental rights. The Lahore High Court agreed, explaining that "climate change is a defining challenge of our time and has led to dramatic alterations in our planet's climate system."[206] For the court, human rights provided the standards by which to assess government behavior, asserting that the "right to life, right to human dignity, right to property and right to information under ... the Constitution read with the constitutional values of political, economic and social justice provide the necessary judicial toolkit to address and monitor the Government's response to climate change."[207] Applying the human rights framework to the allegations of governmental climate inaction, the court ultimately found that "the delay and lethargy of the State in implementing the [climate change framework legislation] offends the fundamental rights of the citizens which need to be safeguarded."[208]

Similarly, the Supreme Court of Colombia considered the government's failure to stem deforestation in the Amazon an infringement of the youth plaintiffs' fundamental rights in *Future Generations v. Ministry of the Environment and Sustainable Development*.[209] Before reaching that conclusion, the court commented on the profound entanglement between human rights

---

[205] See 'CLX Toolkit,' *supra* note 20.   [206] Case 39, ¶6   [207] Ibid, ¶7.   [208] Ibid.
[209] Case 74. The author was a co-counsel in this case.

and the environment and how environmental degradation, which includes climate change, threatens the most fundamental of human rights as it "gradually depletes life and all its related rights."[210]

As this body of jurisprudence has evolved, the characterization of climate change as a major human rights issue has become commonplace. The Philippines Commission on Human Rights, in its seminal *Carbon Majors Inquiry*, spelled out the widespread impacts of climate change on human rights, naming it "the greatest human rights challenge of the 21st century."[211] Indeed, climate change "directly and indirectly impacts the whole gamut of human rights under international law."[212]

The human rights framing of climate change reached its zenith with the Brazilian *Climate Fund* case, where the Supreme Court deemed treaties on environmental law, including the Paris Agreement, as "a species of the genus human rights treaties and [which] enjoy, for this reason, supranational status."[213] In other words, environmental protection – including climate protection – is a core element of human rights law.

4.1.2 Climate Change Presents a Justiciable Question

Over time, though several courts continued to find procedural reasons to dismiss cases before reaching the merits, the majority view shifted such that climate change as a subject matter was not considered off limits for judicial review. Not only are courts not closed to climate issues but there is also increasing recognition of instances in which courts have a duty or obligation to resolve these types of claims. The earliest and still perhaps the clearest articulation of this view can be found in the Dutch Supreme Court's ruling in *Urgenda*. The Court rejected the government's argument that the climate policy is a political issue, that the power to determine GHG emissions cuts lies only with the executive and the legislature, and that, therefore, the matter is off limits for the judiciary. The Court acknowledged that, in principle, this is indeed "a power of the government and parliament" and that "they have a large degree of discretion to make political considerations that are necessary in this regard."[214] However, such power is not unlimited, nor can it be exercised arbitrarily. Therefore, "it is

---

[210] Ibid, pp. 10–11.
[211] Case 1 (*Petition to the IACHR Seeking Relief from Violations Resulting from Global Warming Caused by Acts and Omissions of the United States*, Letter of Dismissal at 1 (Inter-American Commission on Human Rights, Nov. 16, 2006)).
[212] Ibid, at 78 (internal citations omitted).
[213] Case 150 (*Ricki Held, et al. v. State of Montana, et al.*, No. CDV-2020-307 (Mont. 1st Dist. Ct. Aug. 14, 2023)), at ¶17.
[214] Case 29 (*Urgenda Foundation v. State of the Netherlands*, [2015] HAZA C/09/00456689, Judgment at ¶8.3.2 (Dutch Supreme Court, Dec. 20, 2019)).

up to the courts to decide whether, in availing themselves of this discretion, the government and parliament have remained within the limits of the law by which they are bound."[215] Put differently, international and domestic law, including human rights law, set the justiciable boundaries within which the elected branches of government have latitude to determine the details of climate policy.

Courts have asserted this view even in cases where they have found for the respondent government. For instance, in *Friends of the Irish Environment v. Ireland*, the High Court of Ireland held that, "while the court should be vigilant in ensuring that it does not trespass upon the Executive power of State, nevertheless, consistent with its constitutional functions, the court should also be slow to determine that an issue is not justiciable and therefore excluded from review."[216] The Court ultimately concluded that the Irish government had stayed within this margin of appreciation with the climate mitigation policies it established through its National Mitigation Plan.

This does not mean that there is full jurisprudential agreement on the issue of justiciability. For example, some courts in countries such as the United States have tended to take a more deferential approach to policymakers. As we will see in the discussion of standing, in cases such as *Juliana v. the United States*, a majority of judges concluded that courts are not equipped to redress climate harms without impinging upon the realm of political and policy issues that, in their view, is the sole purview of other branches of government.

4.1.3 The "Common Ground" of RCC Law: Ambition and Urgency

As an initial matter, courts tasked with resolving RCC cases must determine what legal norms, doctrines, and frameworks apply to the claims raised. In response, courts have consolidated an approach that is similar to the "common ground" doctrine articulated by the ECtHR. Within the jurisprudence of the ECtHR, the common ground includes not only international human rights treaties but also other "elements of international law," state interpretations of these elements, and state practice reflecting common values.[217] Accordingly, as the ECtHR laid out in *Demir and Baykara v. Turkey*,

> it is not necessary for the respondent State to have ratified the entire collection of instruments that are applicable in respect of the precise subject matter of the case concerned. It will be sufficient for the Court that the relevant international instruments denote a continuous evolution in the norms and

---

[215] Ibid.
[216] Case 63 (*Friends of the Irish Environment v. Ireland*, 2017 No. 793 JR, Judgment at ¶8.3.2 (High Court of Ireland, Sept. 19, 2019)).
[217] *Case of Demir and Baykara/Turkey*, App. No. 34503/97, IHRL 3281, Judgment (European Court of Human Rights, Nov. 12, 2008).

principles applied in international law or in the majority of member States of the Council of Europe and show, in a precise area, that there is common ground in modern society.[218]

In the context of RCC litigation, courts have proceeded in a similar manner to identify the applicable sources of legal norms and doctrines. International and regional human rights instruments have been incorporated into this common ground as well as, interestingly, core features of the international climate regime. Courts have repeatedly identified both the reports of the IPCC and the Paris Agreement as especially relevant sources of law and norms for the adjudication of climate and rights claims. The former represents the best available science on climate change. The latter establishes targets and standards on climate change agreed to by the vast majority of states, in particular the collective temperature target of "holding the increase in the global average temperature to well below 2°C above pre-industrial levels and pursuing efforts to limit the temperature increase to 1.5°C."[219] Together, they provide benchmarks that courts have actively used to understand the scope of state and corporate obligations on climate change.

Crucially, in concrete cases, courts have extracted legally binding consequences from the IPCC and Paris standards even while acknowledging that those standards are not binding per se. In *Urgenda*, for example, the Dutch Supreme Court gave normative power to those sources in determining the "fair share" of GHG emissions cuts that the Netherlands was obliged to contribute to climate action. For the Court, "agreements and rules that are not binding in and of themselves may also be meaningful ... This may be the case if those rules and agreements are the expression of a very widely supported view or insight and are therefore important for the interpretation and application of the State's positive obligations" under the European Convention on Human Rights. As discussed in Sections 1 and 2, translating the nonbinding rules of the global climate regime into binding rules at the domestic level is one of the fundamental roles that the "rights turn" in climate litigation has played in the climate governance regime.

In *Earthlife Africa Johannesburg v. Minister for Environmental Affairs*, for example, the petitioner environmental organizations challenged the South African government's failure to consider climate change impacts in its decision to issue an environmental license for the construction of a new coal-fired power plant. In its 2017 decision, the High Court of South Africa (Gauteng Division) concluded that the government had erred in failing to consider climate impacts and pointed to the UNFCCC as highly relevant to the interpretation of the

---

[218] Ibid, ¶86. [219] Paris Agreement, art. 2.1.a, *supra* note 78.

government's obligations. South African law, according to the Court, had to be "interpreted consistently with international law," which meant that international climate agreements – including specific provisions of the UNFCCC cited by the Court – "are relevant to the proper interpretation" of this core statute of South African environmental law.[220]

The articulation and consolidation of this essential common ground across RCC cases represents a significant convergence of environmental protection, human rights, and climate governance. Indeed, courts around the world have adopted an integrated reading of the international human rights and climate change regimes, recognizing that the relevant norms and doctrines that must guide state and corporate action on climate change emerge from the interplay between these two governance regimes.

Importantly, the ITLOS adopted this integrated approach in its 2024 advisory opinion. ITLOS rejected the argument put forth by high-emitting states – an argument they later reiterated during the ICJ proceedings – that the Paris Agreement serves as *lex specialis* with regard to climate change, thereby precluding the application of other international agreements, such as the UN Convention on the Law of the Sea (UNCLOS), which imposes state obligations for preserving the climate system. Although the advisory opinion focused on UNCLOS, ITLOS's conclusion that the Paris Agreement does not supersede UNCLOS aligns with the common ground doctrine and is likely to be extended by other courts and plaintiffs to human rights agreements.[221]

This approach has given rise to a range of doctrines that address the key challenges of the climate emergency. Before proceeding to the detailed analysis of those doctrines, it is worth highlighting two cross-cutting features that emerge from the integrated reading of RCC law sources: the ambition and the urgency of climate action.

Ambition refers to the scale and depth of action taken to address the climate emergency, including with respect to GHG emissions as well as adaptation to inevitable impacts. The Paris Agreement contains two primary features that speak to the ambition with which states must act. The first is the collective temperature target. The second is the requirement that states act with their "highest possible ambition"[222] – a qualitative statement that helps define the quanta of GHG emissions a particular state is obliged to mitigate. While states

---

[220] Case 55 (*EarthLife Africa Johannesburg v. Minister of Environmental Affairs and Others*, Case no. 65662/16, Judgment at ¶83 (High Court of South Africa (Gauteng Division), Mar. 6, 2017)).

[221] *Request for an Advisory Opinion submitted by the Commission of Small Island States on Climate Change and International Law*; see "Press release 350 (Climate Change Advisory Opinion)," ITLOS. Available at: https://bit.ly/4aqUlf7, at ¶223.

[222] Paris Agreement, *supra* note 78.

are required under the Paris Agreement to report their commitments to climate action – through their NDCs – and are collectively accountable for achieving the Paris temperature goal, individual state commitments to reduce GHG emissions are not legally binding. In other words, the boundaries laid down by the Paris Agreement around ambition are not, by themselves, directly enforceable.

This is where the human rights regime has come into play, reinforcing these boundaries around ambition through the application of legally binding and enforceable state duties. Climate change triggers the gamut of states' obligations to protect and advance human rights as well as redress violations. Courts and quasi-judicial bodies have looked to the international consensus embodied by the Paris Agreement to specify the link between climate change and human rights. Courts and other observers have understood that warming past the Paris temperature target risks impacts and harms so egregious as to be substantively unacceptable from a human rights perspective. This opens the possibility of issuing enforceable remedies that direct governments and corporations to take sufficiently ambitious climate action, including steeper reductions of GHG emissions. By linking the benchmarks set by the climate regime to the enforcement mechanisms of the human rights regime, the latter helps close the accountability gap of the former.

With respect to action on climate change, *urgency* refers to the time frame in which states and others must act. The primary temporal boundary set by the Paris Agreement is the requirement that states' commitments to reduce GHG emissions through their NDCs represent a "progression over time."[223] While providing some guidance as to how state climate action should evolve, it has substantial gaps. For example, within this framework, it would be possible to offload the bulk of emissions reductions to future generations while still representing a progression over time. Human rights norms and law help fill these gaps.

Compliance with human rights duties and norms requires distributing emissions reductions equitably over time and across generations. As with ambition, the human rights regime reinforces the climate regime with regard to urgency, adding specificity to the time frame in which states must act and enhancing accountability to it.

4.2 How Does Government and Corporate Action and Inaction Stack Up to Cognizable Legal Duties?

Having addressed the preliminary questions of framing, justiciability, and sources, I now turn to the ultimate question of RCC cases, that is, whether specific government or corporate actors have complied with their rights-based

---

[223] Ibid.

duties to specific individuals and groups in the context of climate change. In practice, adjudicators approach this high-level question through a multi-step legal reasoning process that examines more concrete procedural and substantive questions. In what follows, I discuss the four questions that are at the heart of RCC cases and that seek to address the unique traits of climate change:

(1) Given that climate change potentially affects everyone, who has *standing* to sue?
(2) Given the myriad actors and factors that contribute to global warming, what is the *responsibility of individual state (and non-state)* entities for climate action?
(3) Given that the temporality of global warming is nonlinear and its worst effects would be felt in the future, *how do state and corporate duties evolve over time*, including those that relate to young people and future generations?
(4) Given the planetary scale of the climate challenge, what is the *geographic scope* of human rights and climate change obligations?

To each of these four questions, I now turn.

4.2.1 Standing

In the early days of rights-based climate litigation, cases would often fail for lack of standing. In recent years, however, courts have increasingly offered analyses of standing that have allowed claims to proceed to the merits. Courts have developed more flexible understandings of the various factors that comprise standing which have increased the likelihood that courts will ultimately recognize standing in a particular case. Nevertheless, many courts still apply a more traditional understanding of this requirement, which means that RCC claims are still not infrequently dismissed due to a lack of standing.

This section will examine how tribunals and quasi-judicial bodies have understood the various components that constitute standing – namely, particularized harm, imminence, and redressability – in the context of RCC cases. Particularized harm refers to the individualized harm a plaintiff in a case must prove they have experienced, while imminence denotes the time frame in which a plaintiff is expected to experience a threatened harm. Redressability, meanwhile, requires plaintiffs to prove that the court is capable of providing a remedy that relieves the harm.

4.2.1.1 Particularized Harm

To prove standing, a plaintiff generally has to demonstrate that they have experienced an individualized harm that distinguishes them from harm that may be experienced by society writ large. This aspect of standing has proven enormously challenging given that climate change has profound society-wide – indeed, planet-wide – implications, though it often impacts certain people disproportionately.

Several courts have found that plaintiffs have failed to demonstrate that they have experienced an individualized (or particularized) harm and therefore do not have standing. For example, the EU General Court and then the EU Court of Justice both reached this conclusion in *Armando Ferrão Carvalho* v. *European Parliament*. In this case, several children and their parents sued the European Parliament and European Council, alleging that EU regulations on GHGs failed to set sufficient reduction targets and were wholly inadequate, thus violating applicable legal obligations, including those stemming from human rights law.

The EU General Court dismissed the case, finding that the applicants lacked standing to sue. The applicants, the court explained,

> have not established that the contested provisions of the legislative package infringed their fundamental rights and distinguished them individually from all other natural or legal persons concerned by those provisions just as in the case of the addressee ... the fact that the effects of climate change may be different for one person than they are for another does not mean that, for that reason, there exists standing to bring an action against a measure of general application.[224]

The applicants appealed to the EU Court of Justice, which affirmed the prior ruling.[225] However, the EU Court of Justice did not rule out the possibility that plaintiffs in other cases, including young people, could demonstrate standing, provided they supply sufficient evidence on the differential impacts that climate change imposes on them and their rights.

This view was echoed in *Smith* v. *Fonterra*. In this case, an Indigenous New Zealander, Michael Smith, sued several high-emitting corporations – including those specialized in dairy production, steel production, and coal mining – claiming that the impacts of GHG emissions stemming from their commercial activities constituted torts. The lower court dismissed the public nuisance and negligence claims but allowed the breach of duty claim to proceed. This finding, however, was overturned on appeal. According to the New Zealand Court of Appeal, that claim also had to be struck out, in part because the plaintiff failed to demonstrate how he was particularly affected by a tortious breach of a duty relative to the general population, as required for the claim to proceed."[226]

---

[224] Case 89 (*Armando Ferrão Carvalho and Others v. The European Parliament and the Council*, Case no. T-330/18, Judgment at ¶¶44–52 (Court of Justice of the European Union, Mar. 25, 2021)).

[225] Ibid, Judgment at ¶¶45–52 (May 8, 2019).   [226] Case 168, at ¶82 (Court of Appeal).

However, as RCC cases have multiplied around the world and climate science and jurisprudence have evolved, courts have developed a more expansive understanding of standing that takes into account the unique nature of global warming. Indeed, a growing number of courts have recognized the existence of particularized harm in spite of the fact that climate change impacts the general population. Often, courts have done this by emphasizing the distinct or disproportionate impact that a plaintiff experiences.

For example, the 2023 ruling in *Held v. Montana* relied on the particular vulnerability of children and young people to climate change to ultimately rule in favor of the plaintiffs, recognizing in the process that mental health harms like climate anxiety were cognizable injuries. In *Held*, sixteen Montana youth sued the state government, arguing that state environmental policies that limited the consideration of climate change in agency decisions violated their state constitutional right to a clean and healthful environment. In its findings of fact, the Montana First Judicial District Court repeatedly noted the mental harms as well as the physical harms experienced by the young plaintiffs. These harms – including the "Plaintiffs' mental health injuries stemming from the effects of climate change on Montana's environment, feelings like loss, despair, and anxiety" – served as the basis for the court's finding that the plaintiffs had sufficiently demonstrated the particularized injuries needed to prove standing.[227]

In even clearer terms, the Belgian judiciary in *VZW Klimaatzaak v. Belgium* emphasized that the widespread impacts of climate change did not negate the possibility of identifying distinct and individual harms as required for standing. In this case, plaintiffs argued that the Belgian government failed to abide by an adequate standard of care and violated its human rights obligations under regional human rights law by virtue of its failure to adequately reduce GHG emissions. In analyzing whether the natural persons named as plaintiffs in the case had standing to sue, the Brussels Court of First Instance recognized that the plaintiffs had a direct and personal interest given the present and future impacts of climate change on their daily lives. That "other Belgian citizens may also suffer their own damage, in whole or in part comparable to that of the plaintiffs as individuals, is not sufficient to reclassify the personal interest of each of them as a general interest."[228]

On appeal, the Brussels Court of Appeal reflected the lower court's finding. One of the defendants claimed that the organizational plaintiff Klimaatzaak

---

[227] Case 149 (*Neubauer, et al. v. Germany*, Judgment at 86–87 (Federal Constitutional Court of Germany, Mar. 24, 2021)).

[228] Case 40 (*VZW Klimaatzaak v. Kingdom of Belgium & Others*, Judgment at 51 (Court of First Instance of Brussels, June 17, 2021)).

lacked an interest that was "personal, direct, certain, born and present" and thus its claims were inadmissible.[229] The appeals court disagreed, finding that the organization did indeed have such a cognizable interest, ultimately rendering the claims admissible. In doing so, the court stressed, as the lower court had, that the direct interest of the individual plaintiffs was not negated by the fact that climate change carries widespread consequences for society at large.[230]

The Administrative Court of Paris echoed the Belgian courts' recognition that cognizable individual injuries are still possible despite the pervasive harms of climate change. In *Notre Affaire à Tous* v. *France*, several environmental organizations sued the French government, arguing that the government violated its obligation under the French Charter for the Environment and the European Convention on Human Rights, among other legal sources, by failing to adopt sufficiently ambitious measures to reduce GHG emissions. In analyzing the admissibility of the claim, the Administrative Court observed that the organizations' mission to combat ecological harm was sufficiently connected to the harm alleged – the excess emission of GHGs and its attendant impacts – to render the claim admissible, although the alleged harm implicates French society as a whole.[231]

The common thread of insight connecting *Held*, *VZW Klimaatzaak*, and *Notre Affaire à Tous* – which is also echoed in the more recent ruling of the ECtHR in *Klimaseniorinnen* – is clear: The general nature of climate change does not prevent courts from recognizing the direct injuries to individuals required for standing.

4.2.1.2 Imminence

Imminence refers to the time frame in which a plaintiff is expected to experience a threatened harm. In general, courts require plaintiffs to demonstrate that a harm – if it has not already occurred – is likely to occur *imminently*. A harm will occur imminently if it will take place in the foreseeable future with limited possibility for intervening action in the interim.

Rather than a purely procedural requirement, courts' assessments of imminence are based on their understanding of how quickly global warming will affect human beings and how quickly those effects will accelerate over time. Crucially, as time goes by and the impacts of climate change become increasingly visible and urgent, courts' views on imminence may shift. In other words, *courts' perception of the temporality of climate change is in itself time-dependent*. As it becomes abundantly clear that climate change is a planetary emergency, courts may be increasingly willing to assert that the resulting harms

---
[229] Ibid.   [230] Ibid, at ¶¶132–135.   [231] Case 84, at ¶¶10–15.

are imminent. Indeed, this is what a growing number of courts have done in their decisions.

In *Neubauer* v. *Germany*, for example, the German Constitutional Court addressed the imminence question by framing the harms alleged by the youth plaintiffs as ones experienced *now* as opposed to far off in the future. The court did that by emphasizing the fact that decisions made now will lock in future limitations that the plaintiffs will experience, which the court categorized as a type of present harm that is experienced by present generations, especially the youth. As the court cogently explained, "the possibility of a violation of the Constitution cannot be negated here by arguing that a risk of future harm does not represent a current harm and therefore does not amount to a violation of fundamental rights."[232]

Meanwhile, in *Sacchi* v. *Argentina*, the UN Committee on the Rights of the Child offered relevant analysis on the relationship between time and harm in the context of climate change, which reflects a more expansive understanding of imminence. In *Sacchi*, a group of youth climate activists filed a complaint with the Committee on the Rights of the Child, arguing that five states – Argentina, Brazil, France, Turkey, and Germany – failed to satisfy their obligations under the Convention on the Rights of the Child by virtue of their contributions to climate change and their failure to take action on it. Though the Committee ultimately dismissed the complaint, finding that the young people had failed to exhaust domestic remedies, it did conclude that the complainants had victim status. In its analysis of victim status, the Committee found that the youth had sufficiently alleged particularized harms resulting from climate change not only as a result of present impacts but also because these impacts were likely to worsen over the course of their lifetimes "if immediate action is not taken."[233]

Another prominent youth-led RCC lawsuit likewise found that young people faced sufficiently imminent harms, as a result of both climate impacts *now* and ones that were likely to unfold in the *future* if the current trajectory remained the same. In *Future Generations* v. *Ministry of the Environment and Sustainable Development*, the Colombian Supreme Court affirmed the youth plaintiffs' right to bring the claim. The Court grounded its conclusion on the "imminent dangers" evident in contemporary climate impacts, including extreme weather events.[234]

---

[232] Case 148 (*Waratah Coal Pty Ltd.* v. *Youth Verdict Ltd. & Ors (No 6)*, [2022] QLC 21, Judgment at ¶¶108–109 (Land Court of Queensland, Nov. 25, 2022)) (internal citations omitted).

[233] Case 115 (*Sacchi, et al.* v. *Argentina, et al.*, Communication Nos. 104/2019, 105/2019, 106/2019, 107/2019, and 108/2019, Decision at ¶¶10.13–10.14 (United Nations Committee on the Rights of the Child, Oct. 8, 2021)).

[234] Case 74 (*Future Generations v. Ministry of the Environment and Others*, 11001 22 03 000 2018 00319 00, Judgment at 11-12 (Supreme Court of Colombia, Apr. 5, 2018)).

On the other hand, some courts have understood the relatively long period of time in which climate harms may elapse as indicative of a lack of imminence. In an early rights-based climate case, the UNHRC found that sea level rise in the Pacific Island of Kiribati did not constitute a sufficiently imminent harm to serve as the basis for a Kiribati citizen's claim of rights infringements resulting from New Zealand's decision to deny his asylum request. It did, however, find that the alleged harm satisfied the imminence requirement for admissibility, characterizing the Kiribatian as facing "a real risk of impairment to his right to life."[235] Yet, in the Committee's analysis of the merits, it articulated a much narrower understanding of imminence in the context of climate change, finding that the ten to fifteen years in which the island may become uninhabitable due to sea level rise was too long of a timeline to constitute a recognizable violation of the right to life.[236]

Similarly, in *Greenpeace Nordic Association* v. *Ministry of Petroleum and Energy*, the Supreme Court of Norway found that the potential climate risk associated with issuing licenses for the extraction of oil and gas in the Barents Sea was too remote to constitute a "real and immediate risk" to the right to life as required under the European Convention on Human Rights. In other words, "the possible impact on the climate will be discernible in the more distant future" and, as a result, "although the climate threat is real, the decision does not involve" a sufficiently immediate risk of loss of life.[237]

Meanwhile, in *Union of Swiss Senior Women* v. *Federal Department of the Environment, Transport, Energy and Communications*, the Swiss Federal Supreme Court adopted a similar view as the Committee, concluding that the alleged climate harms would unfold in the "medium to distant future" and thus lacked imminence.[238] In this case, a collective of elderly women alleged that the Swiss government's failure to put its emissions reductions on a pathway consistent with limiting global warming to well below 2°C violated its obligations under both the Swiss Constitution and the European Convention on Human Rights. In making these claims, the women underscored the particular harms they were exposed to as a result of their age and thus their heightened vulnerability to climate impacts. Using this framing, the plaintiffs argued that they

---

[235] Case 38 (*Teitiota v. New Zealand*, Decision at ¶¶8.4–8.6 (United Nations Human Rights Committee, 2020)).
[236] Ibid, ¶¶9.10–9.12.
[237] Case 51 (*Greenpeace Nordic and Others v. Norway* (formerly *Greenpeace Nordic Ass'n v. Ministry of Petroleum and Energy*), Application no. 34068/21, Judgment at ¶¶167–171 (Supreme Court of Norway, Dec. 22, 2020)).
[238] Case 52 (*KlimaSeniorinnen v. Switzerland* (Formerly: *Verein KlimaSeniorinnen Schweiz v. Bundesrat*), Application no. 53600/20, Judgment at ¶4.4 (Swiss Federal Supreme Court, May 20, 2020)).

suffered sufficiently individualized and immediate harms to render their claims admissible. The Federal Supreme Court disagreed, arguing that the harms of which the plaintiffs complained wouldn't materialize for years, meaning that they were too far off in the future to serve as a basis for the lawsuit. Stressing that, as assumed by the international climate regime, the "well below 2°C" limit established by the Paris Agreement "will not be exceeded in the near future," the court concluded that "the consequences of any global warming exceeding the limit of 'well below 2°C' shall only occur in the medium to more distant future."[239]

Unfortunately, both climate science and everyday experience have shown that the court's assessment of imminence may have been overly optimistic. As GHG emissions have continued to increase, the 1.5°C mark has been surpassed at different moments in different locations,[240] and average global temperatures are likely to blow past it in the early 2030s.[241] Courts, therefore, can be expected to update their views on imminence accordingly.

This is what the ECtHR did in overturning the Swiss Federal Supreme Court's ruling and ruling for the plaintiff association. The ECtHR stated that, in order for the right to life provision of the European Convention on Human Rights to apply to state's climate actions, there needs to be a "real and imminent risk to life." Importantly, the ECtHR acknowledged that the unique features of climate change meant that the approach to standing typically applied in environmental cases required revision – and that the urgency and potential irreversibility of global warming justified granting standing to associations like the plaintiff organization that represent particularly vulnerable sectors of society.[242]

4.2.1.3 Redressability

Redressability refers to the component of standing that requires plaintiffs to prove that the court is capable of redressing the contested harm – that is, providing a remedy that relieves the harm. Though much of whether a court ultimately concludes that the alleged harm is redressable depends on the specifics of the claim and requested remedy, in general courts have taken a split approach in RCC cases in determining whether the asserted harms are redressable.

---

[239] Ibid, ¶¶4.1–4.4 (emphasis added).
[240] See, e.g., M. McGrath et al., 2023 "World Breaches Key 1.5C Warming Mark for Record Number of Days', *BBC*, October 7, bbc.in/3W2BvnW.
[241] See, e.g., J. Hansen et al. 2023. "Global Warming in the Pipeline." *Oxford Open Climate Change* 3 (1); see also R. Lamboll et al. 2003. "Assessing the Size and Uncertainty of Remaining Carbon Budgets." Nature Climate Change 13: 1360.
[242] Case 52, ¶499.

Many courts have understood themselves as capable of providing relief, as a general matter, in the context of rights-based climate claims. Indeed, the very fact that there have been several rights-based climate cases that have proceeded to the merits and wherein courts have ultimately ruled for the plaintiffs means that courts have understood that plaintiffs can satisfy the redressability component of standing in these types of legal claims.

The Irish Supreme Court, for example, in *Friends of the Irish Environment v. Ireland*, clarified that claims concerning whether legislation and regulations stemming from it – including those dealing with climate change – complied with rights obligations were matters of law. As such, they were redressable by the court. This included the case at hand, wherein the plaintiff environmental organization argued that a national climate plan deriving from 2015 Climate Action and Low Carbon Development Act violated rights guaranteed under the Irish Constitution as well as the European Convention on Human Rights, in part because emissions reduction targets outlined in the plan were insufficiently ambitious.[243]

Following a different, more implicit, route, the approach of the Lahore High Court in *Sheikh Asim Farooq v. Pakistan* typifies the way a number of courts have disposed of potential questions around redressability. In this case, the petitioner argued that the government's failure to curb widespread deforestation, including its inadequate implementation of laws and regulations governing deforestation, violated his fundamental rights under the Pakistani Constitution. In its analysis of whether the claim was maintainable, the Lahore High Court answered affirmatively, implicitly recognizing that the court could redress the asserted violations.[244] The tribunal affirmed the plaintiff's standing and ultimately ruled in his favor and directed the respondent government agencies to take measures to implement the relevant laws and curb deforestation.

In the *Held v. Montana* case, the district court judge found as a conclusion of law that the plaintiffs had "proven redressability at trial."[245] During the trial, the youth plaintiffs argued that a state statutory provision preventing state agencies from considering climate change when authorizing projects, including fossil fuel projects, infringed upon their state constitutional right to a clean and healthful environment. According to the court, this alleged harm was indeed redressable, as allowing state agencies to consider climate change in its permitting decisions could result in fewer fossil few projects approved and thus fewer of the GHG emissions driving the plaintiffs' injuries.[246]

---

[243] Case 66, ¶¶6.23–6.27.   [244] Case 81, ¶22.
[245] Case 150 (*Ricki Held, et al. v. State of Montana, et al.*, No. CDV-2020-307 (Mont. 1st Dist. Ct. Aug. 14, 2023), Sec. I(C)).
[246] Ibid, Sec (I)(C)(18)-(22).

Similarly, the Supreme Court of Hawai'i considered the nonlinearity of climate change in *In re Hawai'i Electric Light Company, Inc*, where an energy company challenged the public utilities commission's refusal to authorize the construction of a biomass power plant. The court emphasized the fact that as each year elapses, the chances to successfully avoid climate impacts dwindles, underscoring the need for measures to be taken now. According to the court, "a stepwise approach is no longer an option. . . . The reality is that yesterday's good enough has become today's unacceptable."[247]

This view, however, has not been the rule in RCC cases in the United States. Other courts have found the harms alleged by the plaintiffs to not be redressable because, in their view, there are too many contributing causes to the harm or because the remedy required would extend beyond what the court would be capable of providing. Notably, this was the majority opinion in the ruling issued by the United States Ninth Circuit Court of Appeals in *Juliana v. United States*. In this case, a group of young people sued the US government for its failure to address climate change, arguing that this state of affairs violates their due process rights and requesting that the government pursue decisive actions to reduce GHG emissions and develop a plan to address the impacts of climate change. In the appeals ruling, redressability proved to be a decisive issue. According to the court, the relief requested by the plaintiffs was beyond the authority and capacity of the court to issue and, as a result, the plaintiffs lacked standing.[248]

4.2.2 Individual State and Corporate Responsibility for Climate Action: The Fair Share Doctrine

Greenhouse gases emitted *somewhere* contribute to global warming *everywhere*. This is the essential feature of the climate emergency that renders it a global collective action problem: No single country can reduce GHG emissions enough to prevent dangerous scenarios of global warming without emissions reductions from other countries.

Governments invariably invoke this as a shield against individual responsibility for climate harms. Countries from big (Brazil) to small (the Netherlands) and from high-emitting (United States) to low-emitting (Pakistan) have argued that individual accountability through litigation is inappropriate given that a fundamentally planetary challenge cannot be solved individually. Government defendants typically proffer one or both of the corollaries stemming from this

---

[247] Case 307 (*In re Hawai'i Electric Light Co.*, SCOT-22-0000418, Judgment (Supreme Court of Hawai'i (Mar. 13, 2023)).
[248] Case 41, 22–29.

view: (1) If they stop emitting or reduce their emissions more swiftly, another state or actor will fill the gap (a line of reasoning known as the "drug dealer's defense"); and (2) individual liability is inappropriate because it would only constitute a "drop in the bucket" and thus won't redress the problem of global warming.

As a rebuke to this line of reasoning, courts gradually have developed legal doctrines that affirm individual state and corporate responsibility for climate-induced human rights violations. Specifically, judicial and quasi-judicial bodies have advanced the "fair share" and duty of cooperation doctrines in order to enforce individual obligations to reduce GHG emissions as well as reinforce the collaboration that underwrites the efficacy of the international climate regime. The following sections examine these doctrines in turn.

4.2.2.1 Fair Share Doctrine

States and other actors have historically used the fact that their individual contributions to GHG mitigation will not alone solve the problem to defend against claims seeking judicial enforcement of GHG emissions reduction targets and commitments. Courts increasingly push back against this defense, asserting their own competence to enforce at least minimum contributions to GHG mitigation. Put differently, collective action problems require that relevant actors do at least the minimum: To avoid becoming a free rider, each actor must 'do its part' to contribute to emissions reductions.

One of the earliest and clearest articulations of this principle – the obligation for states to 'do their part,' also known as the *fair share doctrine* – comes from *Urgenda*. In its assessment of the adequacy of the government's mitigation target, the Dutch Supreme Court rebuked the shirking of individual state responsibility on climate change, finding that, among other things, the state's contributions to GHG emissions justified a finding of partial responsibility, which, in turn, meant the state was individually obligated to make a fair share contribution to emissions reductions.[249] Fittingly, the court derives the fair share obligation from the fundamental "no harm principle" in international law. Since the reasoning of the court in *Urgenda* has been widely cited by other courts, it is worth quoting in some length:

> [T]he defense that a state does not have to take responsibility because other countries do not comply with their partial responsibility, cannot be accepted. Nor can the assertion that a country's own share in global greenhouse gas emissions is very small and that reducing emissions from one's own territory makes little difference on a global scale, be accepted as a defense. *Indeed,*

---

[249] Case 29, ¶¶5.7.1–5.8 (emphasis added).

> *acceptance of these defenses would mean that a country could easily evade its partial responsibility by pointing out other countries or its own small share. If, on the other hand, this defense is ruled out, each country can be effectively called to account for its share of emissions and the chance of all countries actually making their contribution will be greatest*, in accordance with the principles laid down in the preamble to the UNFCCC.[250]

Having established that each country has a duty to contribute its share to the fight against climate change, the question that follows is: How to calculate it?

The Dutch Supreme Court looked to the consensus established through the UNFCCC and the best available science of the IPCC to calculate the minimum quanta of emissions reductions with which the state should be expected to comply.[251] The Dutch Supreme Court, moreover, used the concept of the *carbon budget* in order to drive home the point that every additional GHG emission matters.

The German Constitutional Court used the same tool in *Neubauer*. The global carbon budget can be calculated on the basis of the best available science provided by the IPCC as well as the temperature target set by the Paris Agreement. This 'common ground' permits the calculation of the quantity of GHG that can be emitted globally before exceeding the temperature target of the Paris Agreement, namely well below 2°C with all efforts geared towards limiting warming to 1.5°C. Once the global budget is calculated, experts can estimate a particular state's share of that global budget (if a government agency hasn't already) based on historical emissions, consistency with the collective temperature outcome, and other considerations. The domestic carbon budget, which defines the emissions a state ultimately has left to emit, helps quantify the "fair share" of emissions reductions: Emissions that exceed the budget cannot be considered a fair share as they would undermine the ability to limit global warming to approximately 1.5°C.

In France, meanwhile, the Paris Administrative Court also used a carbon budget to ground individual state responsibility for GHG mitigation. In *Notre Affaire á Tous* v. *France*, the court ultimately found the French government liable for exceeding its domestic carbon budget. Though not framed explicitly as a violation of the fair share doctrine, the effect is similar: The state is legally accountable for failing to control its GHG emissions in a manner consistent with acceptable limits to global warming.[252]

In *KlimaSeniorinnen*, the ECtHR endorsed the fair share doctrine as well as the carbon budget approach to calculating it. According to the ECtHR, every state has a human rights obligation under the European Convention on Human

---

[250] Ibid, ¶¶5.7.1–5.8 (emphasis added).   [251] Ibid, ¶7.2.11.   [252] Case 84, at ¶30.

Rights to "do its part to ensure such protection"[253] from the "serious adverse effects on their life, health, well-being and quality of life arising from the harmful effects and risks caused by climate change."[254] A key factor in the ECtHR's conclusion that Switzerland had violated the Convention was the Swiss government's failure to produce a carbon budget against which it could assess the sufficiency of its targets.[255]

Prominent quasi-judicial entities have also implemented the fair share doctrine. As summarized by the Committee on the Rights of the Child in *Sacchi v. Argentina*, "[i]n accordance with the principle of common but differentiated responsibility, as reflected in the Paris Agreement, the Committee finds that the collective nature of the causation of climate change does not absolve the State party of its individual responsibility that may derive from the harm that the emissions originating within its territory may cause to children, whatever their location."[256]

While courts are increasingly likely to find that states cannot hide behind the collective nature of climate change to defend against individually enforceable obligations, not all courts have adopted this stance. The Brussels Court of First Instance, for example, in *VZW Klimaatzaak* v. *Belgium* specifically disagreed with the Dutch Supreme Court's decision to require the Dutch state to reduce GHG emissions by a specific quantity constituting its minimum fair share. The Brussels Court concluded that "it is not for the judge to determine the quantified GHG emission reduction targets for all sectors that Belgium should meet in order to 'do its part' in preventing dangerous global warming."[257]

Significantly, however, this finding was overturned on appeal, as the Brussels Court of Appeal found it appropriately within their purview to set specific emissions reduction targets for the government defendants

> in view of the shortcomings noted in the past and which continue to this day, which can only be corrected by reductions to be planned for the future, in view of the threat posed to the life, private life and family life of the appellants, natural persons, by ongoing global warming [as well as] in view of the importance of maintaining, at the international level, the mutual trust of the State parties to the UNFCCC in the fact that each State will effectively contribute to the global fight against global warming.[258]

---

[253] Case 52 (*Verein KlimaSeniorinnen v. Switzerland*, 53600/20, Judgment at ¶544 (European Court of Human Rights, Sept. 4, 2024)).
[254] Ibid, ¶545. [255] Ibid, ¶¶570–571.
[256] Case 115 (*Sacchi, et al. v. Argentina, et al.*, Communication Nos. 104/2019, 105/2019, 106/2019, 107/2019, and 108/2019, Decision at ¶10.10 (United Nations Committee on the Rights of the Child, Oct. 8, 2021)).
[257] Case 40 (*VZW Klimaatzaak v. Kingdom of Belgium & Others*, Judgment at 82 (Court of First Instance of Brussels, June 17, 2021) (DeepL Translation)).
[258] Ibid, Judgment of the Brussels Court of Appeal, ¶285.

The willingness of courts to issue injunctions and other remedies requiring states to "do their share" of emissions reductions often turns on how the plaintiffs have formulated the goal of litigation. In instances where plaintiffs have alleged a generalized failure of states to act sufficiently on climate change – as opposed to inadequacies in existing legislation or enforcement – courts have expressed an unwillingness to dictate specifically what states must do for fear of judicial overreach. This was the precise finding of the Canadian Court of Appeal in *Environnement Jeunesse* v. *Attorney General of Canada*, which rejected the plaintiffs' request for a finding that the government's inaction on climate change violated their fundamental rights and a remedy commensurate with that finding. According to the court, the plaintiffs ultimately suggested that the court "order 'the implementation of a remedial measure to curb global warming' without further specification."[259] Such a remedy would, however, be "highly problematic" and outside the court's authority to provide.[260]

4.2.2.2 Other Duties to Facilitate Fair Share Contributions

Plaintiffs have sought to hold states accountable to other duties which, though not directly framed as requiring states to contribute their fair share to emissions reductions, nonetheless have the effect of requiring states to act consistently with fair share contributions.

One such example is the *duty of care* deriving from tort law. State officials, according to this line of reasoning, have a duty of care not to act in a manner that would unreasonably harm a certain segment of the population by contributing to climate harms. While this duty is not facially aimed at requiring states to do their share of emissions reductions, it nevertheless would contribute to this in practice by limiting states' abilities to engage in activities, like the approval of fossil fuel extraction, that are inconsistent with the need for states to reduce GHG emissions.

In *Sharma* v. *Minister for the Environment*, the plaintiffs argued that Australia's Minister for the Environment "owes each of the Children a duty to exercise her power under [the Environment Protection and Biodiversity Conservation] Act with reasonable care so as not to cause them harm."[261] This duty of care was, in turn, triggered by the manifold physical and mental injuries threatened by worsening climate change.

---

[259] Case 86 (*ENvironnement JEUnesse v. Procureur General du Canada*, 500-06-000955-183, Judgment at ¶¶9–10 (Court of Appeal of Canada, Dec. 13, 2021)).
[260] Ibid, ¶¶25–32 (emphasis added).
[261] Case 168 (*Sharma v. Minister for the Environment*, [2022] FCAFC 35, Judgment at ¶¶9–11 (Federal Court of Australia, May 27, 2021)).

Initially, the plaintiffs succeeded, as the Federal Court of Australia recognized that "the Minister has a duty to take reasonable care to avoid causing personal injury to the Children when deciding ... to approve or not approve the Extension Project."[262] In reaching this conclusion, the court explained that the duty of care reflected the apportionment of responsibility among multiple contributors, demonstrating a logic similar to that of the fair share doctrine, which also seeks to apportion and hold multiple contributors individually responsible for a shared obligation to reduce GHG emissions. This outcome, however, was short-lived. On appeal, the Federal Court reversed this finding, concluding that there was no such duty of care.[263]

Courts have also interpreted state statutory requirements in a way that, while not explicitly aimed at requiring states to meet minimum fair share obligations, nonetheless helps in practice to effectuate these minimum contributions by preventing activities inconsistent with GHG mitigation.

In *In re Vienna-Schwechat Airport Expansion*, the Austrian Federal Administrative Court found that the construction of an additional airport runway was not in the public interest, given its contribution, among other things, to GHG emissions and thus failed to meet applicable statutory requirements. This finding, however, was overturned on appeal to the Constitutional Court of Austria, which found that the lower court erred in taking into account the relationship of the construction of the additional runway to international climate goals.[264]

4.2.2.3 Duties to Cooperate

Given the interchangeability of GHG emissions, no state acting alone can sufficiently reduce the aggregate level of GHG emissions to avoid warming beyond 1.5°C. In other words, states must work together to ensure collective outcomes are consistent with the overarching goal of avoiding warming beyond 1.5°C.

In this sense, the fair share doctrine can be understood as flowing from the recognition of the need for state cooperation. When states fail to contribute to GHG emissions reductions, it undermines the very possibility of group action. Judicial enforcement of individual contributions acts as a backstop to prevent the unraveling of the state cooperative action needed to ensure the efficacy of the international climate regime.

Courts have also gone beyond this to identify and enforce individual state duties to cooperate, again in recognition of the role such cooperation plays in underwriting global climate action and preventing free riders. One of the more

---

[262] Ibid, ¶¶491.   [263] Ibid, Judgment at ¶¶246–248 (Mar. 15, 2022).   [264] Case 72, at 7–9.

explicit examples of this comes from *Neubauer* v. *Germany*, where the German Constitutional Court advanced a cogent formulation of the duty to cooperate as an essential trait of climate governance. The Court flipped on its head the consequentialist reasoning of the standard government defense – according to which cutting down emissions in any given country would be inconsequential unless other countries do the same – arguing that unless individual states fulfill their own duty to reduce GHG emissions, the trust among states that is essential to the success of climate governance would never materialize.[265]

The Philippines Commission on Human Rights, in its *Carbon Majors Inquiry*, also emphasized that state obligations on climate change include a duty to cooperate, which is essential given the global nature of climate change and the ability of free riders to undermine collective action. In the Commission's view, in conjunction with the *erga omnes* nature of States' duty to protect human rights, the duty to act on climate change is also necessarily implied in each State's duty of international cooperation in addressing human rights issues.[266]

4.2.3 The Evolution of Climate Change: Irreversibility and Intergenerational Impacts

The relationship that climate change has to time has presented a particularly thorny and ongoing challenge for litigants and courts. Climate change compounds over time, with impacts that increase as each year elapses. Thresholds in the climate system, known as tipping points, raise the prospect of widespread ecological damage incapable of reversal in time frames relevant for human beings. GHG emissions are cumulative and themselves potentially irreversible in time frames relevant for the standard human generation – CO_2 remains in the atmosphere for about 100 years before falling to Earth, creating locked-in impacts. And none of this unfolds in a vacuum: To the extent that present action guarantees future outcomes, it is young and future generations – those with the least ability to influence current decision-making – that will experience the brunt of these escalated, locked-in impacts.

All these temporal dimensions of the climate emergency raise serious issues for courts used to adjudicating past or present harms without locked-in distributional effects over time. Indeed, many of the doctrines and tools that courts have developed to assess current and threatened infringements of rights come under serious stress when dealing with the unique temporality of climate change.

---

[265] Case 148, ¶¶201–203.   [266] Case 42.

One such tool is the doctrine of imminence, which was explored earlier in the discussion on standing. In this section, I focus on two other jurisprudential fronts that have sought to address the evolution of climate change over time: doctrines on irreversibility and doctrines on intergenerational justice.

4.2.3.1 Irreversibility

The fact that many climate impacts are effectively permanent – especially the triggering of tipping points within the climate system – has, at times, influenced how courts have resolved climate cases. Notably, the German Constitutional Court's ruling in Neubauer used the irreversibility of impacts to find that the GHG targets laid out by the government had tangible consequences now for the freedoms of young people.[267]

To the extent that litigators and courts have addressed this feature of the temporality of climate change, it often has provided justification for the application of two legal standards: the precautionary principle from environmental law and the non-retrogression principle from international human rights law. The *precautionary principle* provides that when there is reason to suspect that a certain activity will generate serious or irreversible effects, the lack of scientific certainty should not prevent the implementation of measures needed to mitigate those effects. In the context of RCC cases, some courts have noted that the irreversibility of climate impacts justifies the application of the precautionary principle, which typically results in the imposition of a constraint on government or corporate action that contributes to GHG emissions.

The Dutch Supreme Court in *Urgenda*, for example, underscored the relevance of the precautionary principle in understanding the need for suitable measures to tackle GHG emissions, given their implications for the protection of human rights. Indeed, when there arise "real and immediate" risks stemming from global warming, the precautionary principle dictates that measures be taken before such risks materialize.[268]

The *non-retrogression principle* indicates that, once a state has adopted policies to fulfill human rights, it should not backtrack on those measures. In other words, states are expected to follow an upward trajectory in the protection of human rights; whenever they adopt policies or laws that are deliberately retrogressive, they need to prove that they contemplated all alternatives and that the measures were strictly needed to protect other rights and are in accordance with the use of the state's maximum available resources.

---

[267] Case 148, ¶118.
[268] Case 29 (*Urgenda Foundation v. State of the Netherlands*, [2015] HAZA C/09/00456689, Judgment at ¶5.6.2 (Dutch Supreme Court, Dec. 20, 2019)) (internal citations omitted).

In the realm of climate policy, this principle entails that courts "must ensure that governments do not adopt retrogressive measures" with regards to policies that aim to reduce GHG emissions, as the Supreme Court of Brazil held in its ruling in *Climate Fund*. In that particular case, the Court prevented the government's backtracking on the implementation of laws that had established a financial mechanism (the Climate Fund) to support anti-deforestation and other mitigation programs in the Amazon. More broadly, in line with the logic of progressive realization of the Paris Agreement, the non-retrogression principle requires that countries' NDCs be updated upwards as needed in order for them to effectively contribute their fair share to global climate mitigation.

4.2.3.2 Intergenerational Impacts: Distributional Consequences of Climate Change Over Time

The generational implications and inequities of climate change play out most explicitly in rights-based litigation brought by or centering youth and future generations. In the context of these cases, courts have had occasion to address the distributional effects of climate change over time.

Some courts have acknowledged the generational impacts of climate change but have avoided resting their reasoning on harms likely to materialize in the future by focusing on the impacts that young people – who will also endure worsened impacts in the future – are experiencing now.

In *Held* v. *Montana*, for example, the First Judicial District Court of Montana acknowledged that the youth plaintiffs were likely to face climate impacts in the future but focused more closely on the impacts they face now and to which they are disproportionately susceptible as a result of their youth in order to find that the plaintiffs had sufficiently alleged harms traceable to the state's fossil fuel policies. In particular, the court emphasized that children "are at a critical development stage in life" and that all children "are a population sensitive to climate change because their bodies and minds are still developing."[269]

· Less frequently, courts have taken youth-led climate cases as opportunities to advance framings that proactively address how climate impacts are distributed over time. Indeed, one of the most sophisticated articulations of the nexus between constitutional rights and freedoms and time comes from *Neubauer* v. *Germany*. In its decision, the German Constitutional Court found that the government's failure to adequately specify how it would achieve its net zero target in 2050 – a target which itself is constitutionally mandated – risked the possibility that the necessary emissions reductions would be pushed

---

[269] Case 150 (*Ricki Held, et al. v. State of Montana, et al.*, No. CDV-2020-307 (Mont. 1st Dist. Ct. Aug. 14, 2023), at ¶¶105–108).

disproportionately into the future, creating a situation where young people would be forced later on to accede to draconian limitations to their activities in order to achieve net zero emissions. The court's formulation of the relationship between time, climate impacts, and the freedoms of young people represents a significant innovation in RCC jurisprudence. In convincingly defining fundamental rights as "intertemporal guarantees of freedom," the Court held that:

> As ever more of the CO_2 budget is consumed, the requirements arising from constitutional law to take climate action become ever more urgent and the potential impairments of fundamental rights that would be permissible under constitutional law become ever more extreme ... The restrictions on freedom that will be necessary in the future are thus already built into the generosity of the current climate change legislation. Climate action measures that are presently being avoided out of respect for current freedom will have to be taken in future – under possibly even more unfavourable conditions – and would then curtail the exact same needs and freedoms but with far greater severity.[270]

In *Youth Verdict* v. *Waratah Coal*, moreover, the Land Court of Queensland (Australia) advocated for an approach to judicial decision-making in the context of rights-based climate cases that reflected both the intergenerational inequities associated with climate change and the fact that future generations have no way to directly influence present decision-making. This approach should, according to the court, put added weight on the rights of children. The court stressed "the significance of this generation making decisions that could lock-in climate trajectories, the impacts of which will be felt by future children"[271] as well as "an intergenerational imbalance in the effects of climate change itself,"[272] which "makes the rights of children paramount."[273] Such an approach, applied to the facts of the case, indicated that an environmental license for a coal mining project in a sensitive ecosystem should be refused, which the court ultimately recommended.

Similarly, in *D.G. Khan Cement Company Ltd.* v. *Punjab*, the Supreme Court of Pakistan upheld a regulation banning the operation of cement plants – which produce meaningful GHG emissions – in ecologically sensitive areas, basing its decision in substantial part on the need to preserve the climate system for future generations as well as the ability for future generations to meet their needs.[274]

---

[270] Case 149 (*Neubauer, et al. v. Germany*, Judgment at ¶¶120–121 (Federal Constitutional Court of Germany, Mar. 24, 2021)) (internal citations omitted).
[271] Case 148 (*Waratah Coal Pty Ltd. v. Youth Verdict Ltd. & Ors (No 6)*, [2022] QLC 21, Judgment at ¶1580 (Land Court of Queensland, Nov. 25, 2022)) (emphasis added).
[272] Ibid., ¶¶1594–1596. [273] Ibid., ¶1603. [274] Case 111, ¶¶19–20.

This focus on the enormous vulnerability of future generations ultimately led the court to uphold the contested regulation.

Nevertheless, a number of courts utilize understandings of temporality that are not tailored to the specific features of climate change and so tend to gloss over the generational implications and inequities of climate change. And, less frequently, courts have outright denied the existence of generational concerns relevant for the adjudication of climate cases. In the appeal decision in *Sharma v. Minister for the Environment*, for example, the Federal Court of Australia denied that the plaintiff children were vulnerable in a sense relevant for the recognition of a duty of care, noting that the plaintiff children "are in the same position as everyone in the world who is or will be alive at the future times at which the harm is posited."[275]

In *Environnement Jeunesse* v. *Attorney General of Canada*, the Superior Court of Canada echoed this sentiment, finding little basis to focus claims for climate-induced rights infringements, including the right to equality, on persons below the age of thirty-five. Ultimately, the court could not find the "rationality of this maximum choice of 35 years," observing that "facts alleged do not support this choice of 35 years as the limit" and in the end rejecting the articulated class as an "an arbitrary and therefore inappropriate choice."[276]

All in all, youth-led cases have been more unsuccessful than not. It stands to reason from this that courts have, generally speaking, not yet fully incorporated the generational implications of climate change into their legal reasoning. This may, however, change as cases like *Neubauer* v. *Germany*, *Held* v. *Montana*, and *Amazon's Future Generations* continue to establish relevant precedents and their legal reasoning diffuses across jurisdictions.

4.2.4 The Geographic Scope of Climate Change and Human Rights: Territorial and Extraterritorial Obligations

One of the defining features of climate change is that it fails to respect territorial boundaries. GHG emitting activities located squarely within one territory can contribute to climate-induced harms in another territory entirely. This presents a major challenge for RCC adjudication, as courts typically affirm extraterritorial obligations in only a very limited set of circumstances.

In contrast to the doctrines on standing, fair share contributions, and the temporal aspects of climate change, which have all tended to evolve in order to meet the legal challenges of climate change, courts have been more reluctant

---

[275] Case 168 (*Sharma v. Minister for the Environment*, [2022] FCAFC 35, Appeal Judgment at ¶¶338–340 (Federal Court of Australia, May 27, 2021)).

[276] Case 86 (*ENvironnement JEUnesse v. Procureur General du Canada*, 500-06-000955-183, Judgment at ¶¶118–135 (Superior Court of Canada, Dec. 13, 2021)).

and have taken a split approach with regard to cross-boundary effects. Some courts have affirmed state or non-state actors' extraterritorial obligations in the context of climate change, while others have expressed skepticism that such a finding is possible. Meanwhile, other courts have responded to the territorial challenges posed by climate change by focusing their legal reasoning on harms experienced by plaintiffs within the territorial boundaries of the court, in effect avoiding the question of extraterritorial obligations.

4.2.4.1 Extraterritorial Obligations

The existence of extraterritorial obligations is a topic that has been squarely addressed by only a few courts. Notably, international courts or quasi-judicial bodies have been more likely to explicitly affirm the existence of extraterritorial obligations than domestic courts. For example, in the 2017 Advisory Opinion issued by the IACtHR on human rights and the environment, the court confirmed that environmental degradation with transboundary effects – like climate change – can serve as the basis for extraterritorial obligations. According to the Court, "the obligation to prevent transboundary environmental damage or harm is an obligation recognized by international environmental law, under which States may be held responsible for any significant damage caused to persons outside their borders by activities originating in their territory or under their effective control or authority."[277]

Importantly, in *Sacchi* v. *Argentina*, the UN Committee on the Rights of the Child stated explicitly that states could be held responsible for climate-induced harms experienced by children living outside their territorial boundaries. The Committee arrived at this conclusion on the basis of the "effective control" doctrine, whereby the state of origin of the emissions can be deemed to have effective control over them "through its ability to regulate activities that are the source of these emissions and to enforce such regulations."[278]

Meanwhile, other courts have been reluctant to assert legal liability for extraterritorial climate impacts. For instance, the Supreme Court of Norway, in *Greenpeace Nordic Association* v. *Ministry of Petroleum and Energy*, concluded that state obligations on climate change do not extend to fossil fuels produced domestically but combusted abroad, while affirming state responsibility for the consequences of combustion occurring domestically, noting that the right to a healthy environment in the Norwegian constitution "only covers

---

[277] Case 56 (*Advisory Opinion OC-(23/17)*, Judgment at ¶¶101–104 (Inter-American Commission on Human Rights, Nov. 15, 2017)).
[278] Case 115 (*Sacchi, et al. v. Argentina, et al.*, Communication Nos. 104/2019, 105/2019, 106/2019, 107/2019, and 108/2019, Decision at ¶¶10.3–10.09 (United Nations Committee on the Rights of the Child, Oct. 8, 2021)).

the environment in Norway"[279] and that, partly as a result, "each state is responsible for combustion on its own territory."[280]

In *Greenpeace Netherlands v. Ministry of Finance*, Greenpeace Netherlands sued the Dutch government, claiming that its bailout of the airline KLM during the COVID-19 pandemic violated the government's duty of care given the GHG emissions associated with KLM's activities. In the course of assessing the claims put forth by the plaintiff, The Hague District Court denied that the Dutch government had specific obligations stemming from international climate agreements to reduce GHG emissions from cross-border aviation, thereby denying the possibility of a form of extraterritorial obligations.[281]

In one of the submissions included in the *Neubauer v. Germany* case, youth plaintiffs – including one from Bangladesh and another from Nepal – sued the German government, alleging that insufficiently ambitious GHG emission targets in recent climate legislation violated their fundamental rights. Although the Constitutional Court found that the Bangladeshi and Nepalese plaintiffs had standing to bring these claims along with the German plaintiffs, the court ultimately found no violation of a duty of protection.[282] The court based its dismissal of the non-German plaintiffs' requests on the limitations of the German state in contributing to *adaptation* measures. However, it failed to offer a convincing argument against the plaintiffs' other claim: that their rights were violated because of the German state's failure to contribute more decisively to climate *mitigation*, that is, to undertake more aggressive actions and put in place more detailed plans in order to reduce GHG emissions that, albeit originating in its territory, have effects on other countries, especially those like Bangladesh and Nepal that have made the least historical contributions to global warming and yet are experiencing some of its most profound impacts.

4.2.4.2 Focusing on Obligations within Territorial Boundaries

To the extent that an RCC case may raise the question of extraterritorial obligations, some courts have responded by avoiding the issue altogether and focusing on the substantive claims raised by the plaintiffs within the territory in which the courts sit.

For instance, this was the approach taken in *Youth Verdict v. Waratah Coal*, where the Queensland Land Court countered the defendant coal mining company's claim that the transboundary nature of the harm posed by GHG

---

[279] Case 51 (*Greenpeace Nordic and Others v. Norway* (formerly *Greenpeace Nordic Ass'n v. Ministry of Petroleum and Energy*), Application no. 34068/21, Judgment at ¶155 (Supreme Court of Norway, Dec. 22, 2020)).
[280] Ibid, ¶159 (emphasis added). [281] Case 364, ¶4.4 (emphasis added).
[282] Case 148, ¶¶174–181.

emissions rendered the claims nonjusticiable by focusing on the harm that GHG emissions generated by coal produced in Queensland would impose on people in Queensland. According to the court "reliance on the principle of responsibility for transboundary harm is misplaced. The applications are made and will be decided in Queensland, about the mining of coal in Queensland, the combustion of which will cause harm to the environment in and the people of Queensland, wherever the combustion occurs."[283]

This section focused on the fundamental questions and challenges that the climate emergency poses for human rights and climate law. Domestic and international courts as well as UN treaty bodies have sought to rise to the challenge by adapting existing legal concepts and norms to the distinct features of global warming or by developing novel doctrines on complex legal issues, including standing, imminence, non-retrogression, prevention, and extraterritorial obligations. Although far from constituting a consensus, there are clear signs that the global body of law and jurisprudence is gradually converging on a set of core doctrines, including the definition of climate change as a justiciable human rights issue, the existence of rights-based duties of states and corporations to contribute their fair share of efforts to address the climate crisis, the expansion of conventional conceptions of standing and imminence, and the prohibition of retrogressive measures. Other equally important questions remain open, such as the extraterritorial obligations to mitigate and redress climate harms.

As insiders to the law, litigators and adjudicators devote considerable time and energy to the intricacies of legal doctrine. The RCC field is not an exception. The concepts and doctrines analyzed in this section constitute a lively and ongoing dialogue among actors in the field. However, their ultimate goal is to effectuate change in practice, be it in the form of policy or perceptions about the climate emergency. To these issues of impact, we now turn.

5 The Impact of Rights-Based Climate Litigation: Typology and Illustrations

The story of rights-based climate litigation recounted thus far has centered on the emergence and consolidation of the RCC litigation field. Having captured how external and internal developments have acted upon the formation of this field as well as its modus operandi, the analysis now turns to a third, final dimension: impact.

---

[283] Case 148 (*Waratah Coal Pty Ltd. v. Youth Verdict Ltd. & Ors (No 6)*, [2022] QLC 21, Judgment at ¶¶1368–1371 (Land Court of Queensland, Nov. 25, 2022)).

I propose a broad understanding of impact that goes beyond the direct, immediate effects of litigation and captures also the indirect, symbolic effects that oftentimes inform litigants' strategies and courts' decisions and yet rarely appear in media coverage and scholarly analysis. They include not only the concrete policy changes that legal actions seek but also the use of litigation as a storytelling device and as a tool of social and political mobilization.

To that end, I combine the high-level perspective of general trends in the field that I used in the previous section with a more granular analysis of the impacts of four prominent cases: *PSB* v. *Brazil* ("*Climate Fund* case"), *Milieudefensie* v. *Royal Dutch Shell*, *Held v. Montana*, and *Neubauer* v. *Germany*. Given that the RCC field is still young and these cases are recent, the findings on impacts are necessarily preliminary in nature. Rather than offering exhaustive accounts of those cases or extracting definitive conclusions about RCC litigation's effects, the primary goals of this section are to suggest an analytical framework that expands our understanding of the effects of litigation and to illustrate its applications to rights-based climate litigation. As has been the case with more well-established forms of human rights and public interest lawyering that socio-legal scholars have studied over the decades, the passing of time and the proliferation of cases will allow for more robust empirical analysis in the future.[284]

Expanding the analytical and empirical field of vision to include a broader range of impacts is important from both an external and an internal perspective on legal mobilization. From an external viewpoint, the usual focus on the immediate policy outcomes stemming from litigation risks missing crucial facts of the stories that take place after a court ruling, including the latter's impact on public opinion, potential changes in the agendas of governmental and corporate entities that are not involved in the case but who are affected by it indirectly, and the catalytic effect that the case may have on social movements. All these impacts may go in different, even contrasting directions. For instance, as we will see in the study of *Milieudefensie*, the targets of litigation may respond by increasing their contribution to climate mitigation as instructed by courts or by pushing back against or circumventing court orders.

From an internal viewpoint, the goals of participants in RCC cases oftentimes go beyond immediate changes in targets' policy. As interviews with litigators make abundantly clear, indirect changes in other actors' behavior and in the

---

[284] Among the many contributions to this literature, this section draws particularly from McCann, Michael W. 1994 *Rights at Work: Pay Equity Reform and the Politics of Legal Mobilization*. Chicago: University of Chicago Press; Scheingold, Stuart 2004 *The Politics of Rights: Lawyers, Public Policy, and Political Change*. Ann Arbor: University of Michigan Press. For a collective effort at analyzing the impact of human rights litigation, see Malcolm Langford, César Rodríguez-Garavito, and Julieta Rossi, eds. 2017 *Social Rights Judgments and the Politics of Compliance*. Cambridge: Cambridge University Press.

perceptions of the larger public about the urgency of climate change figure prominently in their strategies. On occasion, winning the case on the policy front may not even be the primary goal, as litigators may file a case knowing that, while it has a small chance of succeeding, it may help raise public awareness about or set the agenda on climate action.

Particularly important for many advocates is litigation's storytelling power. "I do think that human rights' greatest strength is its way to tell a story about morality and government responsibility in a kind of general way and the centering of human impacts. It's mostly a storytelling mechanism," said Martin Wagner, Earthjustice's international director and co-author of the Inuit petition. This helps explain why RCC lawsuits have usually been accompanied by sophisticated media strategies that center the human stories behind the lawsuits.

A more nuanced and expansive understanding of impact also aligns with this Element's argument about the contribution of RCC litigation to climate governance. The conventional focus on immediate policy effects lends itself to binary assessments of litigation's contribution. From this perspective, depending on the immediate outcome of the case, litigation either fails or succeeds in advancing climate action. A more skeptical variant of this view holds that, since no single lawsuit or ruling can generate the policy changes that would be needed to adequately address global warming, litigation may be inconsequential even when it succeeds.

Rather than looking for a silver bullet and homing in on direct and immediate impacts, this Element understands RCC litigation as one tool in the highly diverse toolbox of the global climate governance regime. Its contribution to climate governance consists in providing material and symbolic incentives for governments and corporations to speed up and scale up climate action. This requires paying as much attention to the material and direct effects of legal actions and court decisions as to their indirect and symbolic effects.

This section will lay out the four-prong typology structured along two axes: direct–indirect impacts and material–symbolic impacts. From there, it will summarize the four cases that illustrate the kinds of impacts generated by this field of legal practice. The remainder and bulk of the section will thereafter turn to the landscape of impacts produced by RCC litigation over the years.

5.1 Typology of Impacts

In earlier scholarly works, I have proposed a framework that delves into the question of impacts of rights-based litigation and adjudication.[285] This framework draws on well-established literature that has explored the effects of

---

[285] Rodríguez-Garavito, César. 2011. "Beyond the Courtroom: The Impact of Judicial Activism on Socioeconomic Rights in Latin America." *Texas Law Review* 89 (7): 1669–1698, 1669, 1674.

judicial decisions on various societal issues and capitalizes on the strengths of two differing perspectives: neorealism and constructivism. A neorealist perspective, which views law as a set of norms that shapes human conduct, applies a strict causality test to measure the impact of judicial interventions.[286] Thus, a judgment is effective if it has produced an observable change in the conduct of those it directly targets. In contrast, a constructivist perspective, which views laws as a set of mutually constitutive institutions and symbols,[287] applies a range of research strategies to measure both the direct and the indirect impact of judicial rulings. Thus, a judgment is effective even if it does not produce observable changes in the parties to the case; indirect transformations in social relations or alterations in social perceptions are themselves a measurable victory.[288] Adopting a constructivist perspective, the analytical framework I advance considers both direct and indirect effects, whether they be symbolic or material, in order to assess the ramifications of a given case or ruling.

I suggest a four-prong typology that teases out the effects of RCC lawsuits on the basis of their materiality and the directness of their connection to the terms of the case and the judicial decisions reached. In Figure 6, the four-square grid provides a schematic representation of this typology and gives an example of each impact.

Within this schema, *direct effects* refer to actions mandated by the court that alter the conduct of defendants. A typical impact of this sort is the increase in GHG emission cuts mandated by rulings like *Urgenda*. *Indirect effects*, meanwhile, are not specified in court orders but nevertheless stem from the decision and influence the conduct of parties to the case as well as other social actors. For instance, the multi-year mobilization that is needed to take a lawsuit through its different phases can galvanize civil society coalitions pursuing the legal actions; these coalitions can outlive the case and branch out into other forms of advocacy. This was the situation, for instance, in the *KlimaSeniorinnen* case[289] (which boosted and internationalized the plaintiff organization of elderly women and its allies) as well as the *EACOP* case[290] that sought to halt the construction of the East African Crude Oil Pipeline and that, despite the East African Court's initial dismissal of the lawsuit, galvanized a transnational coalition of organizations around the *Stop EACOP* campaign. The legal action metamorphosed into a broader campaign targeting Total, the French energy company behind the pipeline.

---

[286] See Rosenberg, Gerald N. 2023. *The Hollow Hope: Can Courts Bring About Social Change?* Chicago: University of Chicago Press.
[287] See, e.g., Bourdieu, *supra* note 94, 815–816.   [288] McCann, *supra* note 291.
[289] Case 52.   [290] Case 185.

Climate Change on Trial

	Direct	Indirect
Material	Policy design, as mandated by the ruling	Consolidation of civil society coalition
Symbolic	Reframing climate as a human rights issue	Influencing the public's perception about the urgency of climate change

Figure 6 Typology of RCC litigation impacts (adapted from Rodríguez-Garavito, 2011).

Impacts can also be material or symbolic in nature. *Material effects* produce tangible, discretely identifiable changes in the conduct of public or private entities, groups, or individuals. Again, concrete policy changes such as those that resulted from *Urgenda* are prototypical material effects. *Symbolic effects*, meanwhile, involve shifts in ideas, perceptions, and social constructs related to the subject matter of the litigation. As we will see, media coverage of lawsuits can shape public understanding of the underlying issue, producing a symbolic impact.

As Figure 6 illustrates, the intersection of these two axes gives rise to four types of effects: direct material effects (e.g., governmental formulation of a policy ordered by the court); indirect material effects (e.g., consolidation of civil society movements and coalitions); direct symbolic effects (e.g., reframing the issue at play as a rights violation); and indirect symbolic effects (e.g., the transformation of public opinion).

In the remainder of this section, I will use evidence from four case studies to illustrate the general and specific impacts that litigation has had on society and on climate action, in accordance with this four-prong schema. Though each of these cases has been discussed at varying length in previous sections, I begin this analysis with a brief summary of each case to better lay the groundwork for the subsequent discussion on impacts.

5.2 Four Illustrative Cases

The choice of these cases is based on three factors. First, they share traits that permit holding important variables constant, including the fact that they were decided by domestic courts, largely focused on mitigation, and went through the full procedural cycle from the filing of the case to a court's ruling. Second, they differ in key respects that allow for a comparative assessment, including the type of plaintiff and defendant, their legal basis, and the particularities of the domestic legal and political context. Third, they all led to rulings that promote more ambitious climate action. While a more thorough assessment of impacts would include pro-climate action cases that end in rulings for the defendants as well as anti-climate action cases, the nature of this section calls for a more limited focus on a small set of cases with comparable outcomes.

5.2.1 The Climate Fund Case

While in power, the administration of Brazilian president Jair Bolsonaro pursued an aggressive anti-environment agenda. On multiple fronts, his administration attempted to take apart the pillars of Brazilian environmental law while also encouraging the illegal incursion of mining and agriculture into the Amazon forest.[291] One such casualty of this agenda was the Climate Fund, the financial mechanism established to funnel funding to projects and activities that support climate mitigation and adaptation in Brazil. In 2019 and 2020, the Fund laid dormant, as the Bolsonaro administration deliberately neglected to formulate the necessary annual plans and failed to allocate funds. This undercut the primary pathway for the Brazilian government to fund the types of activities that would ensure their compliance with their domestic and international climate commitments.

In response, a coalition of Brazilian political parties, working with NGOs, filed suit against the federal government. In *PSB* v. *Brazil* (the "*Climate Fund* case"), the petitioners argued that the effective freeze on the Climate Fund violated, among other constitutional rights, the right to a healthy environment. According to the plaintiffs, the dormancy of the Fund breached the state's obligations under the Paris Agreement, which requires that states implement measures consistent with the climate commitments they have made thereunder.

On June 30, 2022, the Brazilian Federal Supreme Court ruled in favor of the plaintiffs. The Court found that the government had erred in ignoring a clear mandate of the legislature and had failed to satisfy its constitutional obligation to mitigate climate change through the Climate Fund.[292] Moreover, the state had failed to avoid regression in environmental protection, which further justified judicial intervention.[293] The Court ordered the government to undertake administrative measures to reactivate the operation of the Fund, prepare and present appropriate annual plans for the distribution of the Fund's resources, and refrain from placing new contingencies on resources from the Fund.[294]

---

[291] Watts, Jonathan. 2022. "More Than Two Billion Trees Killed in Four Years. The Amazon Legacy of the 'President of Death,'" *Sumaúma*, September 27, 2022.

[292] Case 151, at 22–33, available at: bit.ly/3y3paYA.   [293] Ibid, p. 21.

[294] Climate Fund Case, *supra* note 299, p. 57.

The political context colors any discussion of the impacts resulting from this decision. Although the ruling was published at the end of the Bolsonaro administration in September 2022, the judgment was not affirmed on appeal until May 2023. By that time, Luiz Inácio Lula da Silva prevailed over Bolsonaro in a highly contested election, marking Lula's third term in the office of the presidency. Lula's ascension to the presidency represented a significant political realignment, including with respect to environmental and climate policy. This political transition shaped the implementation trajectory of the *Climate Fund* case.

5.2.2 Held v. Montana

In the US state of Montana, a paradox at the heart of state environmental policy reigned supreme: A limitation in a state energy policy, the Montana State Energy Policy, expressly prohibited state agencies from considering climate change in their environmental reviews, and yet, a right to a clean and healthful environment is enshrined in the state constitution. Targeting this paradox, in 2020, sixteen youth plaintiffs, with support from OCT, challenged this limitation, alleging that it violated their state constitutional right to a clean and healthful environment by propping up a fossil fuel-based energy system driving the climate emergency. The plaintiffs argued that the state's policy infringed upon their rights to safety and health, as well as their rights to individual dignity and equal protection of the law. Finally, according to the plaintiffs, the state's policy contravened the public trust doctrine by unlawfully depleting essential natural resources like rivers, lakes, wildlife, and the atmosphere.

On August 14, 2023, the Montana First Judicial District Court ruled for the youth plaintiffs. According to the court, the plaintiffs "have a fundamental constitutional right to a clean and healthful environment, which includes climate as part of the environmental life-support system."[295] The policy restricting consideration of climate impacts violates this constitutional right, among others. The court permanently enjoined the policy limiting consideration of climate impacts and permanently enjoined another law (SB 557) barring remedies for challenges based on climate change, as it violated the legislature's duty to provide remedies for the protection of the right to a clean and healthful environment.[296] After the state of Montana appealed the ruling, the Montana Supreme Court upheld it in December 2024.

---

[295] Case 150 (*Ricki Held, et al. v. State of Montana, et al.*, No. CDV-2020-307 (Mont. 1st Dist. Ct. Aug. 14, 2023), Findings of Fact, Conclusions of Law, and Order (Final Order), at 102).
[296] Ibid, at 92, 97–101.

5.2.3 Milieudefensie v. Royal Dutch Shell

Though the global body of rights-based climate cases is still heavily skewed toward those targeting governments, there is a growing subset of cases that seek to address corporate contributions to the climate emergency. One such case is *Milieudefensie* v. *Royal Dutch Shell*, one of the first RCC cases to find that a corporation has enforceable duties to reduce GHG emissions.

In 2019, a group of NGOs and concerned citizens filed suit against Royal Dutch Shell in The Hague District Court, arguing that the company's contributions to climate change violated a duty of care found in the Dutch Civil Code. According to the plaintiffs, this duty of care had to be interpreted in accordance with international human rights law and soft law instruments endorsed by Shell (e.g., the UN Guiding Principles on Business and Human Rights and the OECD Guidelines for Multinational Enterprises). Importing these norms and standards into the duty of care, the plaintiffs argued that Shell's emissions constituted an unlawful act and requested that the Court order Shell to reduce its emissions, among other steps to tackle climate change.

On May 26, 2021, The Hague District Court issued a landmark ruling, agreeing that Shell was required under applicable law to reduce its GHG emissions. The Court found that Shell was obligated to comply with an unwritten duty of care emanating from the Dutch Civil Code, the content of which was informed by the Paris Agreement, the reports of the IPCC, and soft law like the UN Guiding Principles directing corporations to respect human rights.[297] The Court ordered Shell to reduce its emissions by 45 percent relative to 2019 across all of its activities by 2030.[298] To comply with this ruling, the fossil fuel company could draw from Scope 1, 2, and 3 emissions, so long as in the aggregate total emissions were reduced by 45 percent.[299]

On November 12, 2024, however, The Hague Court of Appeal partially annulled the lower court's groundbreaking ruling. Confirming the lower court's finding that Shell indeed has an obligation to reduce its GHG emissions, the Court of Appeal nonetheless held that it could not find, based on the Dutch Civil Code's unwritten and *general* social standard of care, that Shell has an obligation to do so *by a certain, specific percentage*. The Court of Appeal's decision therefore overturned the lower court's provisionally enforceable mandate that Shell reduce its GHG emissions by 45 percent relative to 2019 by 2030. Consequently, Shell and other carbon majors may indeed have an obligation to reduce emissions – but the obligation's scope remains undefined and its enforceability unproven.

---

[297] Case 120, at 4.1.3, 4.4.2.   [298] Ibid, 3.1.1.   [299] Ibid, 4.1.4.

5.2.4 Neubauer v. Germany

In February 2020, a group of German youth lodged a formal legal challenge to Germany's Federal Climate Protection Act with the Federal Constitutional Court, arguing that its failure to adequately specify a 2030 emissions reduction target and a comprehensive pathway to a low-emissions future infringed upon their constitutional rights. Those rights include the right to a future consonant with human dignity and the right to life and physical integrity. Given these alleged infringements, the plaintiffs asked the Court to require the government to set more ambitious emissions reduction targets.

On April 29, 2021, the Constitutional Court issued its ruling which contains one of the most sophisticated analyses of intergenerational responsibilities and duties in the global body of RCC jurisprudence. The Court found that the constitution's "intertemporal guarantees of freedom" prevented present generations from offloading emissions reductions such that younger generations would be disproportionately forced to deal with them in the future.[300]

According to the Court, the constitution requires the government "to treat the natural foundations of life with such care and to leave them in such condition that future generations who wish to carry on preserving these foundations are not forced to engage in radical abstinence. It is thus imperative to prevent an overly short-sighted and thus one-sided distribution of freedom and reduction burdens to the detriment of the future."[301] Having established that the emissions reduction schema established by the legislation threatened fundamental rights, the Court ordered the German legislature to specify emissions reductions for the year 2031 and onward by no later than December 31, 2022.[302]

We now turn to the question at the heart of this section: What are the impacts of rights-based climate litigation? In line with the illustrative nature of this section, the following section is organized by types of impact. I use the distinction between direct and indirect impacts as the organizing grid for the discussion and divide each of those types into material and symbolic impacts. Under each section, I draw on evidence from the four case studies – and, occasionally, from other cases – to illustrate the workings of each type of impact in turn.

5.3 Direct Impacts

Direct impacts are closely linked to the terms of the case, meaning that they implicate the parties to the litigation and relate to the specific issues raised, including, for example, a policy or project targeted for its contributions to climate change.

---

[300] *Neubauer, et al. v. Germany*, Federal Constitutional Court, Decision (March 24, 2021), p. 2.
[301] Ibid, ¶¶193–194.   [302] Ibid, p. 6.

5.3.1 Direct Material Impacts

Among other functions, RCC litigation works to achieve the aims it specifically articulates, meaning in practice the remedies it requests. RCC litigation generally seeks more urgent and ambitious climate measures as well as measures that redress the human rights impacts of climate change, often on particular groups or populations.

Climate science, especially attribution science, has played an important role in shaping the substance of the legal claims articulated and pursued – and thus the material outcomes of cases themselves. This includes with respect to the temperature targets advocates say government and corporate action must respect. Litigators and, consequently, judges tend to use as the relevant standard the temperature target set by the 2015 Paris Agreement, which reflects both the available climate science and political compromise.

Beyond prompting more ambitious climate measures, RCC litigation has served as a tool to translate scientific recommendations into binding legal rules, with material impacts on the standards applied to climate action. Indeed, some involved in the law-science interface have observed a symbiotic relationship between RCC litigation and climate science, noting that they have evolved in relation to each other, as litigation has been structured around advances in science and as science generates increasingly detailed, litigation-relevant insights that many courts have incorporated into their rulings.[303]

Despite some notable victories, not all RCC cases end in rulings for the pro-climate action plaintiffs, which means the impact according to this metric is mixed. But what about cases in which the court indeed issues rulings directing defendant governments or corporations to change their policy or behavior?

The cases detailed in this section all offer insight into this question. In *Neubauer*, the German Constitutional Court ordered the government to set more specific and near-term emissions reduction targets, which it quickly did, in one of the clearest examples of direct material impact on policy in RCC litigation. When the decision was issued, Angela Merkel's administration was coming to a close. As a result, the German media assumed that the revisions to the climate law would fall to the next government;[304] the Merkel administration, however, moved quickly to present a new law that complied with the terms of the *Neubauer* decision.

---

[303] Interview with Delta Merner.
[304] Amelang, Sören et al. 2021. "Landmark Ruling from German Top Court: Key Climate Legislation Falls Short," Clean Energy Wire, April 29, 2021. Available at: bit.ly/3WdsVTc; Justin Worland. 2021. "Angela Merkel Will Leave a Mixed Climate Legacy. Other Leaders Will Fare Far Worse," TIME, May 7, 2021. Available at: bit.ly/3LsFF3J.

Approximately two weeks after the court issued its judgment in *Neubauer*, the federal government unveiled a climate law with revised GHG emissions reduction targets, committing to reducing emissions by 65 percent by 2030 (previously 55 percent) and by 88 percent by 2040 (previously undefined). The revised law also moved up the date for climate neutrality, committing to achieving it by 2045 – five years earlier than initially stated.[305] The new targets laid out by the revised legislation are now also subject to "continuous monitoring" and compulsory bi-annual reporting.[306] By June 25, 2021, the amended law received final approval from the Bundestag and the Bundesrat.[307] To support the goals laid out in the revised law, the federal government approved 8 billion euros in funding for decarbonization and other mitigation measures.[308]

In the aftermath of the Brazilian *Climate Fund* case and also coinciding with the change in administration, the operations of the Climate Fund unfroze – in terms of both the administrative management of the Fund and the actual disbursement of funding for climate projects. Under the Bolsonaro administration and prior to the *Climate Fund* decision, the Managing Committee of the Climate Fund failed to convene for a whopping seventeen months.[309] In stark contrast, the inaugural meeting of the reconstituted Managing Committee was held only eight months into the Lula presidency and a mere three months after the case was affirmed on appeal.[310] In this new era of the Climate Fund, discussions of the Managing Committee – the composition of which has been expanded to include civil society[311] – are grounded in science as well as a broader array of economic, social, and environmental indicators, which allow for more holistic decision-making.[312] Beyond the administration of the Fund, the key metric of impact lay in the disbursement of funding. Prior to the ruling, in 2019, the Managing Committee failed to disburse the entirety of its resources, while the government also declined to allocate any new resources to the Fund.[313] In contrast, during the inaugural meeting of the reconstituted Managing Committee, the president of the Brazilian Development Bank (BNDES) announced a record contribution of R$10 billion to the Climate Fund for 2024.[314]

---

[305] Climate Change Act 2021, Bundesregierung (June 25, 2021), bit.ly/46fBzFt. [306] Ibid.
[307] Ibid. [308] Ibid.
[309] 2020. National Fund on Climate Change (FNMC) Minutes of the 27th Ordinary Meeting of the Managing Committee, Ministry of the Environment, July 15, 2020. Available at: bit.ly/3WsECXL.
[310] 2023. Minutes of the 34th Ordinary Meeting of the Management Committee, National Fund on Climate Change, August 24, 2023. Available at: bit.ly/3y5hXra.
[311] Decree no. 11.549/2023 of June 5, 2023. Available at: bit.ly/3Y6p1y7.
[312] Minutes of the 34th Ordinary Meeting of the Management Committee, *supra* note 318.
[313] Case 151, Initial Petition at 17, available at: bit.ly/4cJVFdC.
[314] Gonzaga, Karine. 2023. "Marina anuncia retomada de captação para fundo clima; expectativa é captar R$ 10,4 bilhões," CNN Brasil, August 24, 2023. Available at: bit.ly/3Wr5PKo.

Milieudefensie v. *Shell* illustrates some of the limitations to the direct material impacts of RCC rulings. In *Milieudefensie*, The Hague District Court ordered Royal Dutch Shell, a fossil fuel company, to reduce its GHG emissions across its various enterprises. Shell did not comply, despite publicly recognizing that "the decision is immediately enforceable against Shell and should not be suspended pending an appeal."[315] According to members of the Milieudefensie litigation team, the tenure of the new Shell CEO, Wael Sawan, was marked not only by noncompliance with the ruling[316] but also an effort to reframe the ruling as riddled with inequities.[317] Indeed, Shell's own documents describe elements of the court's orders as "just not feasible – or even reasonable – to expect Shell, or any single company, to achieve."[318] Moreover, in an apparent effort to double down on its intended noncompliance, Shell announced its intention to move its headquarters from the Netherlands to the United Kingdom and drop "Royal Dutch" from its name only a few months after the lower court ruling.[319] Though these changes were bound up in a larger effort to enhance the appeal of the company's shares, the pressure stemming from the case and changing public opinion also played a significant role.[320] Subsequently, the reversal of the ruling by The Hague Court of Appeal made the issue of compliance moot.

In sum, the case studies demonstrate that RCC litigation can have significant direct impacts on policy. However, the extent to which these policy changes ultimately lead to actual emissions reductions remains an empirical question that has yet to be thoroughly explored in the literature.[321]

5.3.2 Direct Symbolic Impacts

To reiterate, direct symbolic impacts refer to those impacts that center on participants in the case and involve shifts in ideas, perceptions, and social constructs related to the subject matter of the litigation that participants seek to produce.

---

[315] 2022. "Frequently Asked Questions on Dutch District Court Legal Case," Shell, March 22, 2022, at 2. Available at: go.shell.com/4f9zDST.
[316] Interview with Sjoukje Van Oosterhout.   [317] Ibid.
[318] Frequently Asked Questions on Dutch District Court Legal Case, *supra* note 314.
[319] Reed, Stanley. 2021. "Shell Proposes a Shift to Britain, Dropping 'Royal Dutch' From its Name," *New York Times*, November 15, 2021. Available at: nyti.ms/3Y4NzHW.
[320] Ibid.
[321] Some studies have used variables other than emissions in order to quantify the impact of climate litigation on target corporations. See, for instance, Sato, Misato et al. 2024. "Impacts of Climate Litigation on Firm Value." *Nature Sustainability* 7: 1461–1468 (finding that high-emitting firms "experience, on average, a 0.41% fall in stock returns following a climate-related filing or an unfavourable court decision").

5.3.2.1 Reframing Climate Change: Putting a Human Face on Climate Change

Reframing global warming as a human rights issue has been one of the major drivers of RCC litigation. It thus comes as no surprise that litigants in our four cases and in other cases explicitly single out this reframing effect as a direct, intentional impact of their efforts.

In the early aughts, public perceptions of global warming were linked to images like those of polar bears, typically as a stand-in for an environmental framing that focused on impacts to a nonhuman world distinct from the daily machinations of the human one. It was this situation that RCC litigators have sought to disrupt. As Ben Batros, an expert human rights analyst and practitioner put it, "one of the greatest disservices done to the climate movement is that for decades it was portrayed as an environmental problem. Climate change is not an environmental problem, climate change is an everything problem."[322] The lawyers and advocates behind early cases all explicitly sought to put a human face on climate change. For the founder of a leading youth climate rights organization, a central goal of *Held* and other similar cases was "to frame all of these cases on behalf of young people as protecting human rights – bringing the human stories of the harms of climate change to the courts and using foundational laws that are intended to protect people and the resources on which human life depends."[323] Also, for Makoma Lekalakala, one of the advocates behind *Earthlife Africa Johannesburg* v. *Minister of Environmental Affairs*, putting "a human face into policy" was one of the "main missions."[324]

Promoting narrative change and storytelling has been at the core of many RCC cases.[325] To that end, the choice of plaintiff has been crucial. Plaintiffs ground communication of the human impacts of climate change while serving as subjects of moral concern. Sympathetic plaintiffs are also more readily the subject of media coverage, increasing opportunities to push the human framing of climate change into the mainstream.

This helps explain the rise of youth-centered RCC litigation. Children and young people make particularly compelling protagonists, given their heightened vulnerability as well as their widely understood lack of culpability in the climate crisis. "It's important that they are children. They are the ones that will be most harmed, and they are the ones that did the least to harm. My generation and the generations before me are the ones that put the poison into the

---

[322] Interview with Ben Batros, Strategy for Humanity. [323] Anonymized interview (ID#24).
[324] Interview with Makoma Lekalakala, Earthlife Africa Johannesburg.
[325] Matheson, Kelly. 2022. "The Case for Visuals in the Court Room." *Litigating the Climate Emergency*, supra note 19.

atmosphere," as Kelly Matheson, OCT's Deputy Director of Global Climate Litigation, recognized.[326]

That litigation has been successful in reframing climate change as an issue profoundly affecting humans is made evident by the decision of the Brazilian Federal Supreme Court to declare the Paris Agreement a type of human rights treaty in the *Climate Fund* case. Beyond elevating the obligations of the Paris Agreement to the status of domestic constitutional duties, the reframing prompted by this judicial finding has also become an advocacy tool for Brazilian civil society. As noted by Suely Araújo, an attorney with the Brazilian organization Observatório do Clima, "this precedent shows – together with other cases – that the Supreme Court in Brazil cares about the theme of environmental protection. It can be used as an advocacy [tool] in the National Congress" whenever proposed policies threaten to diminish environmental and climate protections. In this sense, Araújo adds, "this precedent can serve as leverage to say to politicians that the Supreme Court is likely to push back on the dismantling [of such] policies."[327]

RCC cases have meaningfully contributed to the reframing of climate change as a grievous threat to humans and human rights; indeed, it is this narrative that now generally dominates public discourse around the climate emergency.[328] As one prominent litigator noted, "we're not talking about the polar bear anymore."[329]

5.3.2.2 Restoring a Sense of Agency

Beyond the specificities of the ruling itself, the judicial process can help shift plaintiffs' and other direct stakeholders' perception of the climate emergency and their sense of agency in responding to it. Lawyers and advocates have observed that the process of challenging governments and corporations on their climate records can restore a sense of agency among plaintiffs. According to *Neubauer* lawyer Roda Verheyen, "the cases are liberating for many people because they feel that there is something that they can do, rather than just stand by and wait; it's empowering."[330]

The heightened perception of agency facilitated by litigation is especially meaningful for youth, among whom climate anxiety fueled by a sense of overwhelm and hopelessness is particularly prevalent. Mat dos Santos, one of the lawyers behind *Held*, commented on the sense of agency the process of taking the stand provided for one of the youth plaintiffs, explaining that the

---

[326] Interview with Kelly Matheson. [327] Interview with Suely Araújo, Observatório do Clima.
[328] See, e.g., interview with Waqqas Ahmad. [329] Anonymized interview (ID#24).
[330] Interview with Roda Verheyen.

young plaintiff has said that "what mattered to me was that I actually had the opportunity to take the stand, and to tell my government, how they were harming me, [...] to have my case heard in that act itself, was truly important to [me]."[331] In another youth-led case, *Sacchi v. Argentina*, filed with the UN Committee on the Rights of the Child, "children and youth groups, the world youth groups or youth groups around the world" were in communication regarding the legal action.[332] This meant that the case "really helped mobilize and empower" despite its ultimate dismissal, according to Ingrid Gubbay, one of the lawyers behind the case.[333] That litigation seeking government accountability for climate action would reduce climate anxiety and foster a sense of agency is consistent with the psychological research on the topic, which identifies taking action as one of the best management strategies for this form of anxiety.[334]

5.4 Indirect Impacts

Beyond the effects on those directly implicated by the case, RCC litigation can shape the conduct and perceptions of a wider audience.

5.4.1 Indirect Material Impacts

Interviews with leading figures in the field make clear that fostering social and political mobilizations is one of the core impacts of RCC cases and rulings. They also show that court rulings may have ripple effects in government and corporate circles that go beyond the parties to the case.

5.4.1.1 Movement Building: Mobilization through Collective Ownership of Litigation

To improve the efficacy of RCC litigation as a tool of social and political mobilization, litigators have taken active steps to enhance the sense of collective ownership over the cases they file. This increases the number of stakeholders directly implicated in the case and whose conduct or perceptions the litigation can influence.

One method has been crowdfunding, which provides opportunities for members of the public to feel personally invested in the case, in addition to supplying needed resources for the case to proceed.[335] This was the approach adopted by the

---

[331] Interview with Mat dos Santos, Our Children's Trust.
[332] Interview with Ingrid Gubbay, Hausfeld LLP.   [333] Ibid.
[334] See, e.g., Hickman, Caroline et al. 2021. "Climate Anxiety in Children and Young People and Their Beliefs about Government Responses to Climate Change: A Global Survey." *The Lancet: Planetary Health* 5 (12): e863–e873.
[335] Anonymized interview (ID#6).

Global Legal Action Network, the lead organization behind *Duarte Agostinho* v. *Portugal*.[336] Litigators have also pursued class actions or otherwise named many co-plaintiffs – even upwards of 20,000 – in order to increase the number of stakeholders invested in the case. The team behind *Environnement Jeunesse* v. *Canada* followed this route, filing a class action on behalf of Quebec citizens under the age of thirty-five, as did the team behind *Milieudefensie* v. *Royal Dutch Shell*, who initially included at least 17,379 individual plaintiffs.[337]

The fact that many involved in RCC cases have cited coalition building and movement empowerment as part of their thinking and litigation design process demonstrates that many have adopted an expansive understanding of the strategic function of RCC litigation. It also suggests that many proponents of litigation are aware of the limitations of court rulings alone, seeking to tie cases to the larger climate movement in order to amplify the inherently limited impact of litigation.[338]

Litigators have at times designed litigation to bolster existing social and political mobilizations on climate well beyond the four corners of the case. Perhaps the clearest illustration of this impact in our sample of cases is *Held*. A lead litigator in the case recounted how the wave of youth-centered climate cases brought by OCT was based on

> the belief that if attorneys could come together and work in a coordinated and strategic way to bring cases that were very similar, rooted in the same kinds of laws and doctrines but tailored for different jurisdictions and that also would be rooted in the best science of climate change and science-based remedies – all on behalf of the youth, that we could create a true movement globally and put pressure on judicial branches in different governments and also start to build precedent where if you had similar enough cases, that they could build off of one another in positive ways.[339]

The aftermath of *Held* demonstrates how political mobilization can be advanced by litigation. For onlookers around the United States, especially youth, *Held* demonstrated that it was possible to challenge state complicity in the climate crisis and win. This has proven to be a source of inspiration for continued action. Indeed, according to Varshini Prakash, a representative of the Sunrise Movement, the *Held* plaintiffs had "proven that Gen Z is a powerful force in the fight against the climate crisis, and we won't be stopped. Mark my words: from courthouses to statehouses to the ballot box in 2024, our generation is taking over."[340]

---

[336] Interview with Gerry Liston. [337] Case 120, *supra* note 305.
[338] Interview with Peter Roderick. [339] Anonymized interview (ID#24).
[340] Smith, Don C. 2023. "Held v Montana: The Beginning of a Climate Change Lawsuit Trend in US State Level Courts or a One-Shot Wonder?" *Journal of Energy & Natural Resources Law* 41 (4): 369–378, 373.

Moreover, rulings like *Held* have mobilized civil society and other actors around implementation. To ensure that the Montana Department of Environmental Quality (DEQ) complies with the ruling, local organizations like the Montana Environmental Information Center have launched public petitions, while individual Montanans have also turned out to protests to pressure the DEQ to fully implement the ruling.[341]

5.4.1.2 Ripple Effects in Government and Corporate Circles: Policy Change, Compliance, and Backlash

According to one media observer, the *Neubauer* decision unintentionally catalyzed a "competition for best climate policy" among Germany's political parties.[342] Save for the ultra-right AfD party, all political parties in Germany took the ruling as a call to action. Framing the decision as a "plea for long-term sustainability and intergenerational justice," the Free Democratic Party called for a complete "restart in climate protection,"[343] which in their view included a clear cap on CO_2 emissions.[344] Meanwhile, hailing the verdict as "epochal" for climate protection and youth rights, Christian Democratic Union Economy Minister Altmaier made clear that the ruling would be implemented swiftly.[345] Even state leaders joined in, seizing the opening afforded by the ruling to advance ambitious state goals. Markus Söder, Christian Social Union Minister-President of Bavaria, the largest state in Germany, called for Bavaria to be climate-neutral by 2040 – well before the existing federal goal.[346]

The federal parliamentary election cycle following the ruling ultimately proved to be the "first in which all of the major parties included climate as an important part of their platforms and ... competed for the mantle of climate leadership."[347] Indeed, this competition for climate leadership created a foothold for smaller parties within the electorate. For the first time, the climate-focused Greens party ran a candidate for chancellor.[348] Climate was at the core of their agenda, which included their proposal "that every federal policy be evaluated in terms of meeting the 1.5°C Paris target for limiting global warming." Their ascent in the

---

[341] Brown, Emily. 2023. "Rally for Climate Action Held in Missoula Following Held vs. Montana trial," KPAX 8 News, October 20, 2023. Available at: bit.ly/3Y8GkP2.

[342] Reitz, Ulrich. 2021. "Union verpasst sich eigene Fridays-Bewegung – Mission: Klima und Kanzleramt retten," Focus Online, May 10, 2021. Available at: bit.ly/4bOG7Un.

[343] Strack, Christopher. 2021. "Verfassungsgericht zwingt Deutschland zu mehr Klimaschutz," DW, April 29, 2021. Available at: bit.ly/4bRWM9A.

[344] "Klimaklage vor dem BVerfG teilweise erfolgreich: Es geht um die Zukunft," LTO, April 29, 2021. Available at: bit.ly/4d6csay.

[345] Amelang, Sören et al., *supra* note 312.   [346] Reitz, Ulrich, *supra* note 349.

[347] Hager, Carol. 2022. "The Shifting Role of Climate Change in the 2021 Bundestag Election." *German Politics and Society* 40 (4): 1–18, 4.

[348] Ibid.

polls indicated that their platform was taken seriously.[349] Ultimately, the Greens joined the governing coalition following the September election. This and their subsequent allocation of significant ministerial authority demonstrates the enduring salience of climate concerns, which the *Neubauer* ruling helped stoke.[350]

Like other types of impacts, indirect effects on governments can work against the intended goals of RCC legal actions. Precisely because they can be consequential for climate policy, some RCC rulings can trigger backlash from governments or political circles that oppose more decisive policies on global warming. Perhaps the clearest illustration of backlash is the resistance with which ECtHR's *KlimaSeniorinnen* ruling was met in the Swiss government and nationalist political circles. Switzerland's Environment Minister played down the impact of the ruling, invoking the referendum on tougher carbon emissions measures that was rejected by Swiss voters in 2021 and declaring that "judges cannot overrule that referendum."[351] Soon after the upper house of the Swiss parliament voted to reject the Court's ruling. The debate on the vote and the text of the declaration made clear that members of parliament were concerned with alleged "inadmissible and disproportionate judicial activism" and Switzerland's "sovereignty."[352] The lower house of the Swiss parliament agreed with the upper house.[353] While the motions were nonbinding and the ultimate decision maker – the Federal Council – was free to break with parliament,[354] the motions signaled the prevailing government sentiment. The Federal Council similarly critiqued the Court's decision but ultimately complied with the Court's deadline and submitted a report to the Committee of Ministers of the Council of Europe detailing the Swiss government's plan to comply. In summarizing the views of parliament, the Council noted "that the judgment goes beyond the limits of dynamic interpretation, that the Court is thereby accepting that its legitimacy is being called into question and that a weakening of the Court's legitimacy could lead to a weakening of the effective protection of human rights in Europe."[355]

---

[349] Ibid.   [350] Ibid.

[351] Francois Murphy. 2024. "Swiss Environment Minister Plays Down Impact of European Climate Ruling," *Reuters*, April 20. www.reuters.com/world/europe/swiss-environment-minister-plays-down-impact-european-climate-ruling-2024-04-20/.

[352] Switzerland Council of the States. 2024. "Statement by the Council of States on the Judgment of the ECHR 'Verein Klimaseniorinnen Schweiz and others v. Switzerland'." June 5. Available at: https://bit.ly/42mQJJi.

[353] "Statement by the National Council on the ECHR Judgment 'Verein Klimaseniorinnen Schweiz and others v. Switzerland'." *Switzerland National Council* (June 12, 2024). Available at: https://bit.ly/3Eewbsa.

[354] Farge, Emma and Dickie, Gloria. 2024. 'Why Does Switzerland's Rebuff of European Climate Ruling Matter?' *Reuters*, June 12. Available at: https://bit.ly/3Wu2cTA.

[355] European Commission, "Communication from Switzerland concerning the case of Verein KlimaSeniorinnen Schweiz and Others v. Switzerland (Application No. 53600/20)" (DH-DD (2024)1123), p. 2. Available at: https://bit.ly/3WrQpVM author's translation).

With RCC rulings becoming more consequential and nationalist opposition to climate action and human rights gaining momentum, similar resistance may arise in response to other RCC legal actions.

The indirect reach of RCC litigation has also extended into the corporate realm, where, for example, the implications of the initial ruling in *Milieudefensie* sent "shock waves to CEOs around the world."[356] Indeed, Milieudefensie, the NGO leading the litigation, received a flood of inquiries following the ruling, including from corporations and law firms seeking to better understand the case and how it may affect them.[357] Private law firms that advise multinational corporations warned of the extensive ramifications that the ruling could have. For instance, Linklaters LLP, a British corporate law firm, predicted that "the case could lead to other types of human rights challenges against corporations by applying the same reasoning to other impacts."[358]

It is too soon to tell what the effects of The Hague Court of Appeal's reversal of the ruling will be. Optimistic observers have pointed to the portions of the District Court's judgment that the Court of Appeal did *not* overturn – for instance, the clear confirmation that protection from dangerous climate change is a human right and the finding that major oil companies like Shell have a "special" obligation to limit CO_2 emissions to counter dangerous climate change. *Milieudefensie* may consolidate jurisprudence linking climate change to human rights and human rights to *private* actors, even if the case ultimately failed to result in a mandatory, specific emissions reduction order for Shell. A more skeptical prognosis would question the continued feasibility of large climate litigation cases following *Milieudefensie*, as the ruling could disincentivize large climate litigation cases and result in a chilling effect. On the other hand, the litigation against Shell has already called attention to the increasingly risky nature of continued investments in oil and gas infrastructure, perhaps paving the way for future climate suits to emphasize shareholder rights and fiduciary responsibilities.

5.4.2 Indirect Symbolic Impacts

For many key players in the RCC field, changing the hearts and minds of the wider public has been an essential motivation for filing suit. This section will examine impacts that are indirect and symbolic in nature: reframing climate

---

[356] Anonymized interview (ID#34); interview with Sjoukje Van Oosterhout.
[357] Interview with Sjoukje Van Oosterhout.
[358] Feijao, Sara. 2021. "Shell Climate Case: Digging Deeper into the Court's Legal Reasoning," Linklaters, June 11, 2021. Available at: bit.ly/3LuXcYV.

change as an emergency in the eyes of the general public and educating the public about the nature of the climate challenge.

5.4.2.1 Framing Climate Change as an Emergency

RCC litigants have viewed the notion that climate change is supposedly a future problem as a roadblock to urgent activation around the issue. In his assessment of why human rights organizations were slow to take up climate change, Pooven Moodley, the former Executive Director of Natural Justice Africa, underscored that part of the issue was that "people have always seen climate change as a futuristic thing that will have impacts later."[359]

By asserting climate-induced violations of human rights that get worse over time, RCC cases have focused the attention of judges and the public more broadly on the now. They have thus contributed to reframing global warming as a problem that is no longer far off but rather an emergency that is on the public's doorsteps.

5.4.2.2 Litigate to Educate

RCC litigation has also served as a tool to educate involved parties as well as the general public on the various facets of the climate emergency. Litigators and other proponents of litigation have cited raising the public profile of climate change as both a motivation for and core impact, or service, of rights-based climate cases. In the *Climate Fund* case, for example, the Brazilian Supreme Court scheduled two days of public hearings prior to issuing its ruling, calling on a variety of government actors, civil society organizations, representatives of the business sector, and research institutes to participate.[360] Those who heeded this call ranged from human rights and environmental groups to persons and organizations engaged in business activities, including the World Bank and Vale S.A., the largest public company in Brazil and the biggest producer of iron ore and nickel in the world. The hearings were broadcast live as well as covered in the media, allowing members of the general public to hear and learn from the testimony of sixty-six different experts.[361]

For those who participated in them, the hearings provided an important opportunity to reach the public through the prism of the most respected judicial body in the country. Making the most of this opening, civil society organizations used the hearings to explain the local relevance of the climate crisis, stress the

---

[359] Interview with Pooven Moodley.
[360] Case 151, Preliminary Ruling on Hearing Convocation (Argument of Non-Compliance with Fundamental Precept 708) (Federal Supreme Court, Aug. 17, 2020), available at: bit.ly/4bRtQij.
[361] See generally, Supreme Court YouTube Channel. Available at: bit.ly/46akPPW.

need for the Climate Fund to operate as intended, and counteract the discourse of climate denial favored by the Bolsonaro administration.[362]

Similar effects are visible in other cases. For instance, by convening three multi-day public hearings in three different locations – Bridgetown (Barbados) as well as Manaus and Brasilia (Brazil) – the IACtHR explicitly sought to offer an opportunity to educate not only the legal community but also the larger public in the details of the impacts of climate change on human rights. Massive participation in the hearings as well as the large audiences that followed the live streaming attest to the impact of this strategy. On the other side of the world, one of the advocates involved in bringing the seminal *Carbon Majors Inquiry* in the Philippines pointed expressly to the opportunity to educate members of the public on climate change – to "laymanize" the problem – as one of the motivations and justifications for filing the petition. Referring to her work with Greenpeace on the *Carbon Majors Inquiry*, she explained that "for us, as a campaigning organization, our main objective is to layman-ize climate justice and bring that to the people on the ground."[363]

The field of rights-based climate litigation has acted upon and shaped the wider world of climate action, producing meaningful changes in policy and framings and fertilizing social and political mobilizations for action on climate change. Yet, for all its achievements, there are clear instances where cases have fallen short and failed to move the needle on climate action. What does that say about the efficacy of litigation?

Clearly, it is no silver bullet. Then again, no single approach to the problem offers a silver bullet, given the profound entanglement of the climate emergency in virtually every major aspect of society from governance and politics to finance to industry and beyond. The contribution of litigation should be seen in the context of the larger climate governance regime. As I have argued in previous sections, RCC litigation should be viewed as a useful albeit limited tool in the larger toolbox that must be brought to bear on this fundamentally wicked problem. From this more modest perspective on the benefits of litigation, the typology and illustrations offered in this section show how rights-based mobilization provides "prods and pleas"[364] for governments and corporations to accelerate and scale up climate action. In this section, I sought to show that those prods and pleas become fully visible only if we broaden our analytical and empirical lens to capture the multifarious direct and indirect, material and symbolic effects of litigation.

---

[362] Interview with Vivian Ferreira (Brazil). [363] Anonymized interview (ID#26).
[364] Ewing, Benjamin and Kysar, Douglas A. 2011. "Prods and Pleas: Limited Government in an Era of Unlimited Harm." *Yale Law Journal* 121 (2): 252–469, 350.

In the following section, I conclude by recapping the argument and delving deeper into the potential and limitations of RCC litigation.

6 Looking Ahead: Lessons, Blind Spots, and the Potential of Rights-Based Climate Litigation

The story of rights-based climate litigation is one of experimentation and unexpected twists and turns. Only two decades ago, the human rights and climate governance fields ran on two quite separate tracks. Not only were there no legal norms that articulated the connection between them but leading actors and analysts in each of these fields were deeply skeptical of the intellectual and practical value of framing global warming as a justiciable human rights issue. At a time when RCC cases are proliferating around the world and garnering considerable media attention, it may be tempting to conclude, with the wisdom of the day after, that this was an inevitable development.

The evidence and the analysis offered in this Element suggest quite the opposite. It took the efforts of many norm entrepreneurs over the years to build the new body of law that litigators and courts are now rapidly replicating and expanding through new cases and decisions. Through an iterative transnational legal process, pioneer environmental organizations and movements and, later, human rights organizations, mobilized existing norms from other fields and proposed new ones to hold governments (and, to a lesser extent, corporations) accountable for climate inaction. Together with a critical mass of supportive governments, they shepherded the many stages of creating "the newest human right"[365] in international law (the right to a healthy environment) and mainstreamed human rights considerations in climate governance, thus "climatizing" human rights.

Many of those norm entrepreneurs would go on to activate and further develop the resulting legal norms through litigation. As courts, UN treaty bodies, and other judicial and quasi-judicial entities have ruled on those cases, a hybrid climate–rights regime has emerged. In broad terms, RCC legal actions (1) take the goals and principles of the climate regime (as specified in the Paris Agreement and IPCC recommendations) as benchmarks to evaluate states' and corporations' climate actions and (2) use the legal standards, mobilizing frames, and enforcement mechanisms of human rights to hold those actors legally accountable to such goals and principles.

In tracing the consolidation of this young field, I sought to offer a more contingent, experimentalist, and process-oriented account of norm creation and

---

[365] 2023. "Amid Daunting Global Agenda, General Assembly President, Opening New Session, Calls on States to Commit towards Advancing Peace, Prosperity, and Sustainability," United Nations, September 5, 2023. Available at: bit.ly/3Y9STcZ.

legal mobilization. In line with constructivist theories of international law and politics, I examined how RCC norms have emerged, how they have been contested and disseminated, and how some of them have cascaded around the world. Although this process is far from complete and many norms and doctrines are embryonic and actively debated, the idea that human rights courts have a role to play in climate governance has gained a taken-for-granted status.

The story of RCC litigation is ongoing. As I write, the Indian Supreme Court has thrown its weight behind RCC jurisprudence by handing down a landmark ruling that seeks to balance the imperatives of a "just transition" toward clean energies, the rights of vulnerable communities, and the protection of a critically endangered and iconic bird (the great Indian bustard).[366] At the same time, in India and other highly vulnerable countries, the profound effects of global warming are no longer a future concern but instead are shaping daily realities and upending the lives of billions of people. In fact, the Indian Supreme Court ruling came down in the middle of an unprecedented heat wave season. I learned about the decision while conducting fieldwork on loss and damage in Bangladesh, working with lawyers and communities in informal settlements and coastal areas during the hottest April ever recorded in the country, which took an undetermined number of lives due to heatstroke. Sharing the feeling of being "inside an oven" which locals throughout South and Southeast Asia reported at the time was a shocking reminder of the depth and urgency of the climate crisis.[367]

It was also a reminder of how little attention RCC litigation has paid thus far to the challenge of compensating vulnerable countries and communities for the harms to which they can no longer adapt and have contributed the least to producing. Indeed, the issue of loss and damage continues to be a glaring gap in the field.

By engaging with both the human rights and the climate governance literature, this Element aimed to capture the two-way process whereby human rights concepts and norms have been challenged and shaped by RCC litigation as much as they have influenced climate governance. Given the early and central role of environmental practitioners and scholars in the field, most of the contributions to the literature have focused on one direction of this relationship, that is, the role of human rights in advancing climate action. I sought to counter this asymmetry by examining the other side as well, that is, how the unique features of the climate emergency have challenged and spurred innovation in human rights law and practice.

In this concluding section, I take a forward-looking approach to the two sides of this transnational legal process. I first recap the Element's conclusions and

---

[366] Case 137, Judgment at ¶29, available at: bit.ly/3LzLegs.
[367] Ratcliffe, Rebecca. 2024. "'Inside an Oven': Sweltering Heat Ravages Crops and Takes Lives in Southeast Asia," *The Guardian*, May 4. Available at: bit.ly/3Lsa4yW.

distill their implications for the climate governance regime. This includes identifying blind spots in RCC litigation that require new legal doctrines and fresh cases and judicial decisions. I then move to extract conclusions from the study's findings on the challenges of RCC litigation for the human rights field and their implications for ongoing debates on the future of the field.

6.1 Climate Governance: Contributions and Blind Spots of RCC Litigation

This Element's broad understanding of legal mobilization's impacts allows us to appreciate the contributions that RCC litigation has made at three different levels. First, it has given rise to a new legal field at the intersection of human rights and climate governance, with its own norms, actors, and modes of operation. The resulting legal corpus comprises norms on some of the most complex questions of climate governance, from who has standing to claim legal protection from climate harms to the temporal and geographic scope of governments' and corporations' duties to reduce GHG emissions and beyond. Albeit still relatively young, the field also exhibits a distinct set of actors who understand themselves as part of an epistemic and professional community, including lawyers, scientists, activists, analysts, funders, and adjudicators. Among the distinctive modes of engagement in the field are frequent collaborations among lawyers, scientists, and social movement organizations as well as the rapid sharing and dissemination of strategies that I have called open-source litigation.

Second, the rise of the RCC legal field, in turn, has generated direct and indirect impacts at a societal level. Direct impacts include the material consequences of judicial orders, such as changes in mitigation targets, as well as the symbolic reframing of climate change and climate policy as a rights issue. Indirect effects include material impacts such as the consolidation of advocacy networks around lawsuits, which oftentimes survive well beyond the conclusion of the litigation and forge new political and legal initiatives to accelerate climate policy. Indirect symbolic effects include longer-term, incremental transformations in the general public's perception of the climate emergency and the immorality of unabated fossil fuel extraction, political inaction, and other drivers of the crisis.

Third, RCC litigation has influenced the working of the two-level climate governance regime. It has effectively served as a mechanism to translate the global normative and scientific consensus on climate change into binding rules at the domestic level. It has done so by creating material and symbolic incentives for governments and corporations to increase the ambition and urgency of their responses to climate change. RCC litigation has become a source of bottom-up pressure to accelerate climate action, thus helping fill to some extent the transparency and accountability gaps that beset the global climate governance regime. Bottom-up pressure has come not only from legal proceedings but also from social movements' involvement in the legal actions as well as in the campaigns that are oftentimes launched in support of those actions.

However, the limits of RCC litigation are as evident as its contributions. There is no silver bullet in the efforts to address the climate emergency, and rights-based legal action is no exception. Given that global warming is one of the most complex planetary problems, it cannot be solved one lawsuit at a time. RCC litigation is only one tool in the toolkit of climate action, one that seeks to complement and catalyze transformations that need to take place through other more capacious means, from international agreements to phase out fossil fuel extraction to domestic policies that promote renewable energy to transnational movements for the protection of forests, oceans, and other key ecosystems on which the stability of the climate system depends.

Moreover, for all its dynamism, the RCC field is strikingly uneven in the attention that actors have given to the bundle of issues that comprise the climate challenge. While they have devoted considerable time and energy to accelerating climate mitigation, they have been less invested in litigation focusing on climate adaptation and compensation. Together with insufficient attention to corporate duties and responsibilities, adaptation and loss and damage are the blind spots that remain as key challenges for the future of the field.

The dearth of cases on *adaptation* is particularly striking, given that it lends itself more naturally to a human rights frame. Adaptation refers to the measures needed to protect communities from the locked-in impacts of climate change, including, for example, the building of sea walls in areas expected to experience sea level rise. The absence or insufficiency of adaptation measures, therefore, can be shown to have direct, localized impacts on specific individuals and groups – for instance, coastal communities impacted by sea level rise. This, in turn, can help litigants prove standing, causality, and rights violations in a more straightforward way than in mitigation cases. At a time when a survey of IPCC scientists shows that 94 percent of respondents estimate that humanity will blow past the 1.5°C target and is headed for a "semi-dystopian future, with famines, conflicts and mass migration, driven by heatwaves, wildfires, floods and storms" of increasing frequency and intensity,[368] the need for more ambitious and urgent adaptation measures will increase dramatically. In this context, it is

---

[368] Carrington, Damian. 2024. "World's Top Climate Scientists Expect Global Heating to Blast Past 1.5°C," *The Guardian*, May 8. Available at: bit.ly/4cJeJJ1.

likely that RCC legal action on adaptation will multiply apace, thus playing a role similar to the function it has played in the realm of mitigation.

In order to develop the necessary norms and remedies, litigants and courts can draw on important precedents such as *Daniel Billy* v. *Australia*, a petition filed by a group of Torres Strait Islanders against the state of Australia with the UNHRC for its failure, among other things, to implement timely adaptation measures to protect the islands they inhabit. The Human Rights Committee agreed with the Islanders, finding that Australia's "failure to adopt timely adequate adaptation measures to protect the authors' collective ability to maintain their traditional way of life, to transmit to their children and future generations their culture and traditions and use of land and sea resources discloses a violation of the State party's positive obligation to protect the authors' right to enjoy their minority culture."[369]

Climate compensation constitutes another major gap both in climate governance and in the international human rights system. Despite the rising salience of loss and damage after COP26 in Glasgow, international negotiations have failed to make tangible progress on the establishment of a financial mechanism to compensate vulnerable countries and communities for the harms to which they can no longer adapt, from forced displacement to lost income to noneconomic harms like deep dislocations of cultural and family life. Therefore, further expansion and updating of human rights standards and tools are needed to address climate change's domestic and global distributive dimensions. To that end, litigants and courts will have to address head-on the extraterritorial impacts of climate change. This is an issue that remains largely underdeveloped, as even otherwise innovative tribunals like the German Constitutional Court in *Neubauer* have dodged it.

Given that, by definition, transnational climate reparations are issues of global economic redistribution from the Global North to the Global South, and that Northern countries have long stalled or underfunded negotiations and institutional mechanisms on loss and damage, this issue should become a major concern in RCC litigation and the climatization of rights more broadly.[370]

In addition to the cases analyzed in previous sections, litigants and courts dealing with compensation claims can draw on the legal doctrines advanced in ongoing cases. Particularly promising are *Asmania* v. *Holcim* (where plaintiffs are seeking compensation from and a declaration of accountability against a major Swiss building company for climate impacts in Indonesia) as well as

---

[369] Case 125, ¶8.14 (emphasis added). See Voigt, Christina. 2022. "UNHRC is Turning up the Heat: Human Rights Violations Due to Inadequate Adaptation Action to Climate Change," EJIL: Talk!, September 26, 2022. Available at: bit.ly/4cM8rIw.

[370] Wewerinke-Singh, Margaretha. 2023. "The Rising Tide of Rights: Addressing Climate Loss and Damage through Rights-Based Litigation." *Transnational Environmental Law* 12 (3): 537–566.

Municipalities of Puerto Rico v. *Exxon Mobil* (where Puerto Rican cities are seeking compensation from the fossil fuel corporation, alleging that the latter's emissions and intentional misrepresentation of climate risks have violated Puerto Rican citizens' human rights).[371]

Finally, a major gap in RCC litigation concerns *corporate accountability*. The vast majority of rights-based climate cases target governments, despite a recent uptick in cases naming corporations as defendants. As a result, the RCC case law on corporations is underspecified. This blind spot mirrors that of human rights law writ large, which is considerably more capacious in holding states accountable than in spelling out the duties owed by corporations and the remedies for corporate human rights violations. This is still the case despite important developments in the last decade, including the UN Guiding Principles on Business and Human Rights (UNGPs).[372]

As future RCC litigants and courts continue to turn their attention to corporate actors, they can draw from three promising legal developments in the field. First, while rights obligations and international climate obligations are typically not directly binding on corporations, some courts have interpreted the RCC normative "common ground" – established by human rights and climate change jurisprudence as well as the international climate regime – to develop a more expansive understanding of corporate duties. The most notable precedent in this regard is the decision of The Hague District Court in *Milieudefensie* v. *Shell*. The Court found that Shell was required to comply with an unwritten duty of care – informed by the international climate regime as well as human rights norms – which ultimately meant that it was required to achieve certain GHG emissions reductions. Importantly, the Court applied the UNGPs as "a global standard of expected conduct for all business enterprises" to determine the content of Shell's duty of care. Although The Hague Court of Appeal overturned the remedy in this case, it upheld the underlying rationale that companies like Shell have a "special obligation" to reduce GHG emissions.

Second, litigants have proactively sought new venues for complaints that help flesh out corporate responsibility for climate harms. For instance, a number of complaints have been filed with OECD contact points. The OECD Guidelines for Multinational Enterprises on Responsible Business Conduct are soft law recommendations from governments to multinational corporations on responsible and sustainable business practices.[373] The specific guidelines on

---

[371] Cases 297, 311.
[372] Deva, Surya. 2021. "Business and Human Rights: Alternative Approaches to Transnational Regulation." *Annual Review of Law and Social Science* 17: 138–158.
[373] OECD, 2023 Guidelines for Multinational Enterprises on Responsible Business Conduct, Sec. IV, ¶¶1–5, p. 25, June 8, 2023. Available at: bit.ly/3LsSvyT.

human rights provide a hook which organizations have attempted to use to hold corporations accountable for the human rights implications of climate change and prompt corporate climate action.[374]

Third, courts have made use of procedural requirements – including citizen participation obligations as well as Indigenous people's right to free, prior and informed consultation and consent – to directly or indirectly constrain corporate behavior and activities that contribute to climate change. A useful precedent for future cases of this sort is *Sustaining the Wild Coast* v. *Shell*, whereby community members and organizations challenged Shell's plans to conduct seismic surveys for fossil fuels off the eastern coast of South Africa. The plaintiffs requested an interim interdict to prevent Shell from proceeding with their planned surveys before the final resolution of the case, which the High Court of South Africa ultimately granted. In coming to that conclusion, the court emphasized the consultation obligations for which Shell was responsible and with which it failed to comply.[375] Though the court did not address the ultimate climate ramifications of Shell's exploration activities, the decision has the practical consequence of making such activities – and their resulting climate contributions – less likely by enforcing procedural rights which delay, potentially indefinitely, their start.

6.2 The Future of Human Rights: Lessons from RCC Litigation

The story of rights-based climate litigation vividly displays the potential as well as the shortcomings of human rights concepts and strategies in dealing with the existential challenges of the Anthropocene, from climate change to biodiversity loss to toxic pollution. The evidence presented in this Element shows how human rights analysts and practitioners were initially blindsided by the climate emergency. When the lawyers in pioneer RCC cases reached out to human rights organizations, they were met with a mix of indifference and disbelief. At the time, most human rights actors conceived of climate change as an abstract issue that was best left to scientists and environmentalists. For some major international organizations like HRW, the lack of interest in global warming stemmed from an entrenched attachment to a set of tools and tactics that led them to miss emerging fundamental challenges to human rights that fell outside their tunnel vision. Since the multicausality and planetary scale of climate impacts (as well as the key role of fossil fuel companies in causing them) did not lend themselves easily to the time-tested tactic of "naming and shaming" individual governments into compliance with human rights, for more than a decade the leading actors in the field took a back seat in the development of RCC law and action.

---

[374] See, e.g., Cases 96 and 112.   [375] Case 247, Interim Judgment of 28 December 2021, ¶68.

They were not alone in waking up late and struggling to deal with the unprecedented complexity of global warming as a legal issue. Courts and quasi-judicial bodies also grappled with lawsuits and petitions that pushed the limits of human rights law and concepts. Designed as they were to deal mostly with backward-looking accountability for acts that could be clearly attributed to individual actors, human rights norms and theories offered only limited guidance to adjudicators dealing with the nonlinear temporality, entangled causality, and planetary nature of extreme weather events, tipping points, and massive extraterritorial impacts. In response, domestic and international tribunals as well as UN treaty bodies have gradually developed forward-looking interpretations of key legal concepts and doctrines in human rights law, including the justiciability of planetary harms, the responsibility of individual states and corporations, and the status of victim. In terms of Iris Young's helpful distinction, they have thus complemented the traditional "liability model of responsibility" with a future- and solution-oriented approach to human rights.[376]

The evolution of the human rights theoretical and legal repertoire in response to the climate emergency is far from finalized. While law changes slowly, global warming is accelerating dramatically. If human rights are to remain relevant for mitigating, adapting to, and compensating for climate harms, future RCC cases and decisions will need to deepen the evolution of human rights law in time-sensitive, future-looking, and planetary-scale directions. With the Paris Agreement's framework facing a critical juncture – marked by its failure to deliver results and increasing co-optation and resistance from the fossil fuel industry and anti-climate action governments – the human rights field must move beyond Paris to help address the resulting political and legal void. As it has done in other areas, it can offer mechanisms that uphold the truth and focus attention on human suffering, responsibilities that the Paris framework appears increasingly unable to fulfill.

More broadly, the story of RCC litigation offers insights for ongoing discussions on the future of human rights as the field celebrates the seventy-fifth anniversary of the Universal Declaration of Human Rights. The rise and consolidation of the RCC field offers empirical evidence of the continued dynamism and experimentation in the human rights movement. The findings in this and other studies[377] stand in stark contrast with the premature announcement of the "endtimes" of human rights[378]

---

[376] Young, Iris Marion. 2011. *Responsibility for Justice*. Oxford: Oxford University Press; Sikkink, Kathryn. 2020. *The Hidden Face of Rights: Toward a Politics of Responsibility*. New Haven: Yale University Press; Rodríguez-Garavito, *supra* note 19.

[377] See, for instance, Dancy, Geoff and Fariss, Christopher J., *supra* note 13; Sikkink, Kathryn. 2017. *Evidence for Hope: Making Human Rights Work for the 21st Century*. Princeton: Princeton University Press.

[378] Hopgood, *supra* note 13.

that have consumed a considerable amount of airtime in some academic circles, especially in the Global North.

To my mind, a useful step toward a generative dialogue about the future is to get over the debate on the supposed demise of human rights. A whole ten years have passed since the publication of Stephen Hopgood's book on the "endtimes of human rights."[379] While Hopgood and others put their finger on real issues of inequality and strategic stagnation within the human rights movement, his argument rested on thin empirical evidence and had important analytical blind spots, as I have argued elsewhere.[380] A decade later, what seems to have stuck is the book's provocative title rather than its more nuanced arguments.

I suggest we turn the page and embrace the end of endism in human rights. The best available evidence shows that, after ten years, the end of human rights mobilization has failed to arrive.[381] It has certainly failed to arrive in the realm of climate governance, where advocates, tribunals, scientists, social movements, Indigenous peoples, youth activists, and regular citizens have increasingly turned to human rights frames and tactics to accelerate climate action.

None of this is to deny the formidable challenges that human rights values and norms face in a time of ecological emergencies, war, technological disruption, democratic backsliding, geopolitical tension, and rising inequalities. Nor is it meant to imply that the human rights field's traditional concepts, tactics, and narratives are adequate to deal with those challenges. Indeed, as I have sought to show, they need to be considerably revamped if human rights are to remain relevant in the coming decades.

In pointing in this direction, this Element contributes to recent literature on international human rights that focus on agency, experimentation, and possibilities for hope.[382] Recentering hope and looking toward the future would be a helpful way to celebrate the seventy-fifth anniversary of the Universal Declaration of Human Rights and think about the next seventy-five years, when the worst effects of climate change will be felt unless deep and urgent transformations take place in economy, politics, and culture.

The response to endtimes pessimism is not facile optimism. As Rebecca Solnit explains in concluding that it is not too late to take decisive climate

---

[379] Ibid.
[380] Rodríguez-Garavito, César. 2023. "Human Rights at 75: The End of Endism," Open Global Rights, December 1, 2023. Available at: bit.ly/3Wc5SIt.
[381] Dancy, Geoff and Fariss, Christopher J. 2023. "Human Rights Are Still in Demand," Open Global Rights, July 3, 2023. Available at: bit.ly/3ScgshD.
[382] See, among others, de Búrca, Gráinne. 2021. *Reframing Human Rights in a Turbulent Era*. Oxford: Oxford University Press; and Sikkink, *supra* note 389; Rodríguez-Garavito, *supra* note 70. For an insightful analysis of this literature, see Çali, Basak. 2024. "Optimism in International Human Rights Scholarship." *American Journal of International Law* 118 (2): 374–387.

action, "hope is not optimism. Optimism assumes the best, and assumes its inevitability, which leads to passivity, as do the pessimism and cynicism that assume the worst."[383] While we feel the pain of the loss of human and nonhuman lives and livelihoods around the planet, we also know that "to hope is to recognize that you can protect some of what you love even while grieving what you cannot – and to know that we must act without knowing the outcome of those actions."[384]

---

[383] Solnit, Rebecca and Young Lutunatabua, Thelma, eds. 2023. *Not Too Late: Changing the Climate Story from Despair to Possibility*. Chicago: Haymarket Books.
[384] Ibid.

Acknowledgements

This book is the result of a five-year professional journey that took me to a wide array of venues where climate litigation and advocacy unfold – from international and domestic courtrooms and diplomatic summits to civil society meetings and grassroots communities in countries as diverse as Australia, Bangladesh, Brazil, Egypt, Germany, Kenya, South Africa, the Netherlands, the United Arab Emirates, the United States, and beyond. My first debt of gratitude goes to the judges, advocates, movement leaders, diplomats, and other key actors of rights-based climate litigation who generously shared their time and insights with me through interviews and conversations. Without them, this book – and indeed the field of rights-based climate litigation – would simply not exist.

As anyone who embarks on a long journey knows, it would not have been possible without the certainty that comes with having a home. NYU School of Law and its Center for Human Rights and Global Justice provided not only a supportive home base but also the nourishing scholarly and advocacy community that made this project possible. I am particularly grateful to my colleagues at the Climate Law Accelerator (CLX) and the Earth Rights Research and Action Program (TERRA). Melina De Bona, Carlos Andrés Baquero-Díaz, Emma Crowe, Youssef Farhat, Ashley Otilia Nemeth, and Yoyo Wong provided essential research and organizational support. Importantly and generously, they believed in CLX and TERRA when they were only ideas in my mind and helped turn them into the dynamic and generative action-research spaces they are today. I owe a special and deep debt of gratitude to my colleague Jacqueline Gallant, whose exceptional analytical talent, wizardry with words, and immensely generous spirit were crucial at every step of the research and writing process.

I benefited greatly from the encouragement and insightful comments of participants in the many events and workshops where I presented the findings and arguments of this book. I am particularly thankful to the nearly 30 colleagues who generously commented on the full manuscript at the two workshops CLX organized for this purpose at the University of Amsterdam and NYU Law in late 2024. In my effort to bridge the climate law and human rights fields, the support and encouragement of Philip Alston, David Boyd, Gráinne de Búrca, and Kathryn Sikkink were essential, as always. Equally important was the financial support of the FILE Foundation and the Open Society Foundations, which made it possible for this Element to be published open access, making the digital version freely available for anyone to read and reuse under a Creative Commons licence.

No matter how long the journey or how far the destination, home is where the heart is. For me, that's wherever Ulpi is. This book is dedicated to her.

Sustainability: Science, Policy, Practice

Series Editor-in-Chief
Arun Agrawal
University of Michigan

Arun Agrawal is Samuel Trask Dana Professor in the School for Environment and Sustainability at the University of Michigan. His research focuses on the political economy of human-environment interactions and systems, sustainability of social ecological systems, governance of natural resources, inter-temporal and cross-scale dynamics of socio-environmental changes, and the effects of climate change on conflict and health outcomes.

Advisory Editorial Board
Neil Adger, *University of Exeter*
Anthony Bebbington, *The Ford Foundation*
Christoph Béné, *Alliance Bioversity International*
William Clark, *Harvard University*
Ruth S. DeFries, *Columbia University*
Melissa Leach, *University of Sussex*
Diana Liverman, *University of Arizona*
Yadvinder Malhi, *University of Oxford*
Debra Rowe, *Oakland Community College*
B. L. Turner II, *Arizona State University*
Esther Turnhout, *University of Twente*

Editorial Board
Vanesa Castan Broto, *The University of Sheffield*
Paul J. Ferraro, *Johns Hopkins University*
Reetika Khera, *Indian Institute of Technology Delhi*
Myanna Lahsen, *Linköping University*
Christian Lund, *University of Copenhagen*
Johan Oldekop, *University of Manchester*
Laura Vang Rasmussen, *University of Copenhagen*
Diana Ürge-Vorsatz, *Central European University*

About the Series
This series showcases scholarship that investigates persistent, multi-scale challenges to global sustainability and strategies to address them. It facilitates the consolidation of the science and social science of sustainability, bridging the gap between knowledge, policy, and practice. It aims to include the best reviews of themes central to environment, development, and sustainability.

Cambridge Elements

Sustainability: Science, Policy, Practice

Elements in the Series

Girl Power: Sustainability, Empowerment, and Justice
Jin In

Climate Change on Trial: Mobilizing Human Rights Litigation to Accelerate Climate Action
César Rodríguez-Garavito

A full series listing is available at: www.cambridge.org/ESBL

For EU product safety concerns, contact us at Calle de José Abascal, 56–1º, 28003 Madrid, Spain or eugpsr@cambridge.org.

www.ingramcontent.com/pod-product-compliance
Ingram Content Group UK Ltd.
Pitfield, Milton Keynes, MK11 3LW, UK
UKHW020112281225
466395UK00014B/217